ANANCY
IN THE
GREAT HOUSE

ANANCY IN THE GREAT HOUSE

Ways of Reading West Indian Fiction

JOYCE JONAS

Foreword by Houston A. Baker, Jr.

Contributions in Afro-American and African Studies, Number 136
Henry Louis Gates, Jr., Series Editor

GREENWOOD PRESS
New York • Westport, Connecticut • London

Library of Congress Cataloging-in-Publication Data

Jonas, Joyce.
    Anancy in the great house : ways of reading West Indian fiction /
Joyce Jonas.
        p.   cm.—(Contributions in Afro-American and African
studies, ISSN 0069-9624 ; no. 136)
    Includes bibliographical references.
    ISBN 0-313-27344-8 (lib. bdg. : alk. paper)
    1. Caribbean fiction (English)—History and criticism.   2. Harris,
Wilson—History and criticism.   3. Lamming, George, 1927-   —
Criticism and interpretation.   4. West Indian fiction (English)—
History and criticism.   I. Title.   II. Series.
PR9205.4.J66   1990
813—dc20   89-25880

British Library Cataloguing in Publication Data is available.

Library of Congress Catalog Card Number: 89-25880
ISBN: 0-313-27344-8
ISSN: 0069-9624

First published in 1990

Greenwood Press, 88 Post Road West, Westport, CT   06881
An imprint of Greenwood Publishing Group, Inc.

Printed in the United States of America

The paper used in this book complies with the
Permanent Paper Standard issued by the National
Information Standards Organization (Z39.48-1984).

10 9 8 7 6 5 4 3 2 1

Contents

Foreword

Post-Colonial Talk and the Critic as Anancy

There is a way of talking about the world today that is, at best, tricky. On one hand there is "plain speaking," which generally means enunciation by consensus, talking to a traditional assembly that believes that words can not mean exactly what just anyone wants them to mean. The plain speakers are historically rooted in the belief that an identifiable point in a solidly discernible past, an essential and discoverable *goodness*, *truth*, and *beauty*, became inscribed in books that remain *great* for all seasons and climes.

The plain speakers mock all attempts to amend or emend *great* texts as willful perversity at worst--and misguided or faddish enthusiasm, at best.

Facing off against plain speakers are adherents of the order of the trickster. These adherents are, as it were, the "other" hand in today's talk.

The order of Anancy is the special branch of liminal energy that is most forcefully occupied by the author of the present study. The spider/spirit spinning out webs of signification that are anything but plain, simple, enduring, empirically verifiable--this is the nature of agency where Anancy is concerned. Anancy's web is homespun out of the stuff of one's own being-in-the-world; it is also a fine-spun catch of sensibility that takes in every air-borne particle. Hence, the web is a place and space of hybridity that creates, by its very presence in the world (which is often invisible, unseen, a gossamer of the margins) new combinations and juxtapositions.

Where talk is concerned, Anancy's web is like the vertical intersecting sonics of melancholia, rebellion, or revolution, erupting through the linear spaces of hegemony. Anancy talk is thus, a discourse outside the normal or traditional precincts of the historically valorized and hegemonically inscribed good, beautiful, and true.

It is not, however, merely a counter semantic weight on the balance of definitions and meanings.

Rather, it is, as I have already suggested, a hybrid sounding of everything blowing about on land and seascapes of the globe. It is a transnational catch of signifiers and signifieds--spinning--always producing new formations.

If there are poles between which the web is spun or suspended, they are the transient markers of "betwixt" and "between."

Betwixt and between what?

Well, that is precisely the nature of liminality, isn't it?

The "between" is, as Victor Turner and others have suggested, precisely the ground for the examination (even the reification) of old customs and beliefs, but also the territory where a "return" to primary materials of a culture reveals new possibilities. One suspects that for the very astute initiand, the "return" also reveals the very *constructivist* nature of culture itself--and one's self as initiand.

So there is about and abroad these days this new trickster/unplain talk creating new formations. Voices--very brilliant and critical voices from the margins--are spinning collaged messages. They are re-visionist voices from the nooks and corners of valorized spaces. Their catches of texts come sometimes from unheard places--the Caribbean in its trans-American fullness, for example.

In the present study, Professor Joyce Jonas provides a stirring instance of Anancy as critic. Her quite extraordinary close readings of unheard volumes from the Caribbean are infinitely useful, but what makes her readings in themselves so productive is that they are functions of a replicable model. What Professor Jonas has created is a trickster's hybridity of method, bringing together symbolic anthropology, philosophical insight, sociopolitical observation, literary exegetical expertise. The result is a fresh interpretation of the Caribbean writer and his text, catching old plantation arrangements in its webs only to deconstruct them through a finely-spun and perceptively filtering margin of analysis.

George Lamming and Wilson Harris and their respective *oevres* are well served by the liminal criticism of Professor Jonas. For she shows us that for artists as deeply imbricated in the economies of colonialism, immigration, and hegemonic language-overdetermination as Lamming and Harris, only a tricky and powerful model will serve our comprehension. It is as though there have been myriad significations floating all along in the works of these two brilliant Caribbean writers awaiting a critic's web sufficient for their catch. The critical home for these significations that Professor Jonas constructs is a trickster's gift to us all--full of productive potential for the traditionally unheard--thoroughly disruptive of old orders of plain speaking. Professor Jonas's text ushers in, it seems to me, a new world of thoroughgoing critique for New World spaces.

Since, however, I have been so closely allied to her project, and since I am such a thoroughly persuaded listener to her Anancy talk, I can not claim objectivity with respect to her present work. Of course, if I did claim such a posture, I would be in violation of the very undergirding claim of her study. For it is precisely a myth of objective and historically verifiable truth that Professor Jonas is about the tricky business of deconstructing. She wishes to demonstrate that it is not so much that language holds the web of culture together as the fact that language is itself the *only* web available *as* culture. Hence the privilege and ability to spin one's own tale (and refuting, in the bargain, the myth of one's tail, as someone has stated it) is the primal task of culture bearing--witness bearing to our *hereness*. But I do not want to rehearse the argument of Professor Jonas's study in this preface--in part because Professor Jonas's eloquence is so much keener with respect to her project than any I could spin.

But if I am compelled to give up the task of summary along with any claim to objective evaluation, still I would like to make claims in the realm of feeling and affect. I can say that Professor Jonas's study is a web in which I feel all of us who are devoted to a new order of speaking can take pleasure--intellectual, emotional, and political. For her Anancy talk captures the "other" hand in ways that are enormously and joyfully liberating.

Houston A. Baker, Jr.

Acknowledgments

My thanks are due to the many friends and colleagues who made this work possible. In particular I wish to express sincerest gratitude to Professor Houston A. Baker, Jr., whose patient and incisive criticism of the manuscript at each stage of its production proved invaluable. To my dearest friend, Peggy Laramee, I extend warmest thanks, for without her practical assistance in the form of child care, and her emotional and spiritual support, I would have abandoned the project long ago. My husband, Pryor, has been a tower of strength and encouragement throughout, and my children Marion, Timothy, and Martin were the inspiration that kept me going.

Studying the works of these two authors has been a wonderful growing experience; I wish to thank Wilson Harris and George Lamming for this gift to the world of their creative labor.

Thanks are also due to Faber and Faber, Ltd., for permission to quote extensively from *Palace of the Peacock*, *The Whole Armour*, and *Genesis of the Clowns*. Quotations from *In the Castle of My Skin*, *Natives of My Person*, and *Season of Adventure* are reprinted with the author's kind permission. Martin Carter graciously gave permission to quote from his *Poems of Affinity*, and the quotation from E. K. Braithwaite's *Islands* appears by courtesy of the Oxford University Press. Part of Chapter II was first published as an article in Callaloo 35 (Spring 1988), and is reprinted here in revised form by kind permission of The Johns Hopkins University Press.

Readers who have firsthand experience of life in a Third World country may know how many additional problems are faced by the would-be writer--an irregular electricity supply, unreliable mail services, and the high cost of reproduction being the more obvious hurdles. I must therefore thank Dawn and Faye for their heroic determination to complete the typing, and their patience during the process of editing. A word of appreciation is also due to the University of Guyana and the University of Pennsylvania for their joint sponsorship of my research activities.

Thanks are finally due to Professor Henry Louis Gates, Jr. for the interest he has taken in this book as the Greenwood Press Series Editor, and to Dr. James Sabin, Executive Vice President of Greenwood Press, for his patience and support during the long and problem-fraught period of preparing the manuscript for publication.

Any errors, omissions, and infelicities are all my own.

Joyce Jonas
University of Guyana

ANANCY
IN THE
GREAT HOUSE

Introduction

Among the most exciting philosophical concepts to have emerged in the twentieth century is the notion that in any inquiry the object under scrutiny is, in fact, prefigured and preconstituted by the perceptual frame. Whatever the academic discipline, pure objectivity seems always and inevitably to elude us. Even in the natural sciences it has been established that findings are determined by the viewing apparatus, which, in turn, is a function of the kinds of questions asked. To complicate matters still further, developments in linguistics suggest that both our perceptions and our communication of those perceptions are more or less subject to the delimiting constraints of language. We are, it seems, forever trapped in metaphors--prisoners of the word--though paradoxically language is the very vehicle of expressivity offering release into authentic being.

The three chapters in this volume examine the related problems of language and perception as thematic motifs in the works of two Caribbean novelists, Wilson Harris (b. British Guiana, 1921) and George Lamming (b. Barbados, 1927). In particular, they discuss "imperialist" habits of perceiving and naming the world and analyze the techniques employed by both authors to demystify the imperialist "text," and thus transform a landscape formerly colonized by the word. The novels selected for analysis are Wilson Harris's *Palace of the Peacock*, *The Whole Armour*, and *Genesis of the Clowns*, and George Lamming's *In the Castle of My Skin*, *Season of Adventure*, and *Natives of My Person*.

My project is to offer a tentative method of reading Caribbean texts in such a way that their concern with language and perception is laid bare. To this end, the anthropological concept of liminality is brought to the service of literary explication. Two icons are employed: the Great House and Anancy, the trickster figure of West Indian folklore. The Great House names a colonial worldview of binary oppositions: black/white, exploiter/exploited, First World/Third World, capital/labor, technology/nature, male/female. Anancy represents the suppressed energeia of such a formulation--a deconstructive energy that finds expression through the artist.

The mode of reading that I propose invites the reader to focus on the margins and boundaries of and within each of the six novels selected and to decode the colonized landscape, reaching beyond rigidly fixed premises to alternative world views. In such a reading the artist (both the author and the reader within the text) is found to function as a shaman, leading protagonists and readers alike through a rite of passage into new perceptions and insight. Both Lamming and Harris, I will show, insist on the reader's active participation in a deconstructive rewriting of texts. Such an activity is made possible by a variety of formal techniques that I have named "anancy-strategies" in honor of the muse of these two writers.

Throughout Africa and the African diaspora in the New World, folktales are told of the trickster Anancy--half-spider, half-man--who, though perennially in tight situations, is singularly adept at turning the tables on his oppressor and emerging more or less unscathed. His ability to extricate himself lies in his gift with words, his talent for spinning yarns. In African mythology, Anancy is a god, responsible for creation itself, though his kindness to humans has brought his fall from the favor of Nyame. In disfavor with Nyame, the supreme sky god, he finds himself positioned between earth and heaven.

The image of the spider on its web is, it seems to me, a fine symbol of the artist at work--creating a whole world from his own substance. Like Anancy, the artist escapes the disastrous prospect of nonbeing by weaving a (fictive/narrative) thread and climbing it to freedom. He takes the strand of linearity (oppressive history or plot) and complicates it by making a patterned web of connections and interrelationships--a woven "text" that turns history/his story into oracular myth, an infinite play of signifiers.

The spider-creator as icon for the Caribbean artist, supplies, too, the concept of exile and of interstitiality--of a strong, yet frail, creation suspended between, and drawing together, separate worlds. Such complexity, ambiguity, and limitless dialogue as are suggested by the web's interwoven strands and its essential impermanence stand in sharp contrast to my second icon: the House of the word. Imposing and immovable, the House brings with it fixed notions of inside and outside, above and below. It names a polarized landscape of exploiter and exploited, enlightened and benighted, Prospero and Caliban. Such an arrangement, while giving authority to the owner of the word, appears (but *only* appears) to dispossess all that lies beyond its architectural premises.

While the icons of Anancy and Great House derive from a Caribbean context, my anthropological orientation is owed to scholars such as Mary Douglas, Arnold van Gennep, Victor Turner and Claude Levi-Strauss. In particular I use Douglas's concept that what we name "dirt" is merely a function of structure--a dangerous liminal region lying beyond accepted premises. Van Gennep's discussion of the "pivoting of sacredness" where boundaries meet is similarly crucial. From Victor Turner's work I borrow insights into the social dialectic of structure and antistructure and carnival moments of social "communitas" where preconceptions and customs are reassessed and revised.

My Anancy figure thus speaks of a dialectical relationship. Each of the texts in this study is profoundly encoded with a Caribbean experience: each resists the House-folk polarizations of an exploitative capitalist system, asserting instead relationships, mutuality, dialogue. Each of the novels, too, engages the reader as a participant in the "writing" of the text by means of literary techniques that make reading a highly selfconscious activity. For common to all six novels is this major feature: that attention is drawn to the possibility of multiple readings of reality. In *Palace*, two alternative readings are rendered through Donne and his half brother narrator. In Genesis, Frank Wellington revises his own original reading and estimate of his companions. In *The Whole Armour*, the narrative repeatedly oscillates between visions of deprivation and of rich blessing. The same pattern emerges in Lamming's work. In *Castle*, events of chronological time are reread in a revisionary activity that gives meaning as well as purpose to what had appeared a catastrophic defeat. In *Season*, Fola views the world first from a Eurocentric perspective, then from the point of view of the exploited folk. And in *Natives*, the texts of male European historians and ideologies are juxtaposed with "leaves" of memory kept by a feminine and silenced community of the dispossessed.

Focusing, then, on the liminal--the boundaries, crossroads, marketplaces--the first of these three essays examines the polarized worldview (House-plantation) of Eurocentrism and the dangerous "dirt" lying outside and beyond its imperialist architecture. Lamming's *Season of Adventure* (1979) and Harris's *The Whole Armour* (1962) are seen to present such a colonized landscape, laid out by the authors in order that it can be deconstructed.

In the second chapter, while continuing the liminal approach, I concentrate more specifically on the role of the artist as "edgeman" promoting dialogue at the thresholds and crossroads of a colonized world. Juxtaposing Lamming's *In the Castle of My Skin* (1970) with Harris's *Genesis of the Clowns* (1977), I explore the carnivalesque energeia that subjects the fixed premises of the House to ironic questioning, mercilessly parodying the sacred tenets of authority's word. The recurring phenomenon, in all six novels, of the artist-reader within the text is here examined in detail.

Finally, in the third chapter I blend with the anthropological concept of liminality a feminist perspective, thus widening the discussion to embrace problems of women's oppression, class exploitation, and postindustrial destruction of the environment. The binary oppositions created by the word now are seen to include male-female, culture-nature, technological progression-ecospheric destruction. Great House assumptions that have in turn led to epic conquest, imperial rule, technological mastery, and now Star Wars--are here exposed as barren concepts that alienate humanity from itself, producing division within the very psyche. Using two novels of conquest--Lamming's *Natives of My Person* (1972) and Harris's *Palace of the Peacock* (1960), I discuss this phenomenon of the divided self by way of the pun "I-eye," which provides scope for the polysemous existential debate on the need for a marriage of the phallic "I" (bespeaking action, the rational, the material) to the womblike "eye" (bespeaking reflection, imagination, the spiritual). In a word, the West Indian colonial experience, as presented by the two novelists, is examined not for its social realism, but as an anagogic discourse on the mythic profundity latent within historic events.

The artistic strategies of Lamming and Harris avoid fixed premises and insist on dialogue with other texts and with readers; indeed they even go so far as to name the reader as the very writer of the text! Their technique lays siege to the presumed authority and opacity of language by an omnipresent wordplay of pun and irony. It creates resonant images by a careful juxtaposition of event or character. It may, rather than mirroring reality, create a world where conventional boundaries are lost and certainties eroded, where, in fact, what is mirrored is the reader himself, caught in the very process of "framing" the text. Silences may well be more voluble than words, as the writers give preeminence not to structures (plot, character, and climax) but to metaphor, to resonances between juxtapositions, and to vibrations set up through intertextuality and allusion.

By laying bare the very process of perception, and by extension, the role of the reader of the text, both Harris and Lamming imply the need for a dialectical paradigm. Theirs is a vision of a world in which relationships are the necessary ground of being and interstitial spaces where minds meet, the very womb of a new world vision. These two novelists bring to their art a long tradition of Anancy tales, calypso satire, playful punning that erodes the defining power of the word, strategies of deception, and, above all, a creative spirit that can turn deprivation into plenitude, empty spaces into echoing chambers. The Anancy artist is the masquerading carnival figure par excellence, celebrating play in a structured world that threatens momently to destroy what is most precious in the human spirit.

I

Beyond the Great House

During the 1950s and 1960s the sparse trickle of novels that flowed out of the Caribbean swelled to a steady stream, a stream that continues to grow in immensity and volume. Two of the most prominent figures of the modern renaissance in Caribbean fiction are Wilson Harris, born in Guyana (then British Guiana) in 1921, and George Lamming, born in 1927 in Barbados. The novels of these two writers are, at first glance, vastly dissimilar. Harris's prose is densely textured, highly allusive, and close to poetry in its rhythms, its play with the sounds and meanings of words, and its many-layered imagery. Evidently the product of a wealth of reading and erudition, Harris's novels prove daunting to the newcomer--especially in the author's flouting of novelistic conventions. Lamming's novels, by contrast, are less experimental. But while they are accessible, they are also rich in associative imagery and symbol. Harris's metaphysical bent further complicates his fiction, while Lamming's concern with topical sociopolitical issues gives his fiction an added immediacy. I juxtapose these two very different artists to illustrate a common topography characterizing West Indian fiction. This topography might be called the "plantation landscape."

A brief view of Caribbean settlement patterns serves to clarify this phrase. In the eighteenth and nineteenth centuries, wherever Europe established colonies in the New World, a peculiar structuring of the landscape occurred, namely the emergence of a Great House and a surrounding plantation. This spatial ordering left its mark. The spectacle is of a proud monumental edifice--dwelling place of beauty, culture, and wealth--surrounded by a cultivated land and enslaved workers whose very existence was a function of their relation to the Great House. It was, of course, the labor of the workers that produced the Great House's wealth.

Anthropologists assert that societies order their physical surroundings in ways that ritually express a sense of cosmic order. If this is so, then the landscape constituted by the Great House and its surrounding exploited land and laborers can be examined for its underlying cosmological implications. The plantation model is one of a bounded landscape that ritually gives pride of place to Eurocentric attitudes and values while sweeping away all that is non-European (African, Indian, Arawak) as so much polluting "dirt." A perpetual outsider vis-a-vis the Great House and its sacred boundaries, the West Indian native has historically experienced deprivation and rejection. Further, since his traditional culture was scorned by the occupants of the Great House, his self-respect and dignity were constantly subject to erosion. The indoctrination resulting from the divided landscape was so insistent and effective that even a writer of V. S. Naipaul's insight and ability could come to agree with a European judgment that West Indians are lacking in creativity.[1]

In the divided world expressed in the ritual inside/outside, white/black, master/servant structuring of the plantation landscape, the West Indian artist becomes an edgeman--one inhabiting the margins of social structure. This is particularly true of the writer, since the language he works with is the "gift" of the colonizer, while his message and interest arise from the folk. The novel as art form is a western product, but narrative technique may well have an indigenous flavor. From the writer's vantage point as outsider, the task is to deconstruct and criticize dominant social structures. Yet social criticism is not his sole (or even his principal) aim. For his premier and most radical function is to invert the extant social structures so that the center of sacredness located formerly in the Great House is now relocated among the houseless folk. In such a rearrangement, folk creativity and vitality take precedence over the various forms of European tradition. As presented by Lamming and Harris, therefore, the artist functions as shaman, as the trickster of universal folklore, who leads his audience away from a structured world into a place of disorientation--a ritual marginality. In the marginal or liminal regions, there is both room and material for the creation and expression of a uniquely West Indian worldview. The margins of the House are transformed into the limen (threshold) of a new world. Here, the artist as shaman-trickster recounts myths of origin--sacred stories that, in Eliade's words, "have constituted [the folk] existentially." Such stories explain the folk's "legitimate mode of existence in the Cosmos."[2]

The intended readership of West Indian fiction is primarily

the West Indian himself, yet both Lamming and Harris clearly achieve a vision that is at once particular and universal. The novels that will be examined in this study are two-edged in their effects. At the sociopolitical level they criticize neocolonials who have, as it were, taken up residence in the Great House of Eurocentric values. Concomitantly, they celebrate and, more importantly, articulate, the folk heritage that survived--in some instances even flourished--beyond the boundaries of the Great House. At still another level of Lamming's and Harris's fiction, the House becomes a metaphor for Western thought, valorization of material progress, empiricism, and capital accumulation. The silent folk, by contrast, come to symbolize yearnings of mankind that remain unsatisfied by such Western glorifications. At the psychoaesthetic level of interpretation, the plantation landscape as it is negotiated by Harris and Lamming stands as an icon for the ongoing dialectic between ordered yet limited perception and the creative disorder of art. The artistic process, of course, has been seen variously as the ordering of chaotic experience, as the introduction of disorder among falsely structured perceptions, and as a dialectic of both order and chaos. In *Man's Rage for Chaos*, for instance, Morse Peckham argues that man "desires above all a predictable and ordered world,"[3] and suggests that the scientific modus operandi seeks supremely to identify such order. Art, in contrast, he sees as an impulse to disorder, manifesting the properties of innovation, disruption, disorientation, and formal discontinuity. By ceaselessly exposing its audience to a disruption of normal expectations, art provides healthy stimulation of our creative capacities. In Peckham's formulation, "art is rehearsal for the orientation which makes innovation possible."[4]

Within the plantation landscape, though, reference to the "innovation, disruption, disorientation and formal discontinuity" necessary to creative innovation immediately introduces the political dimension. To engage in creative activity in the Caribbean necessarily implies a political engagement, and technical innovation by the novelist is inevitably an implicit ideological statement. In the profoundest sense, the Caribbean novelist is a revolutionary.[5]

The foregoing definition of art as part of a dialectical process that is politically charged and revolutionary in character is latent within the anthropological approach that I bring to a reading of these novels. Certainly, the employment in preceding paragraphs of terms such as "boundaries," "liminality," "structure," and "ritual" betray an anthropological orientation, and, indeed, succeeding discussions will draw quite explicitly from the insights of symbolic anthropology. Victor Turner's model of society as a dialectical process of structure/antistructure is vital to the analysis that follows as is Mary Douglas's *Purity and Danger*, a salient study that discusses the sense of "sacredness" that attaches to social structure and the corresponding "danger" (and power) abounding at society's margins.[6]

Since both Lamming and Harris are responding critically to given structures--to authorized texts, as it were--their vantage point is necessarily that of antistructure. They explore a middle ground, a liminal zone lying "betwixt and between" a dominant, fixed structure and a rejected tenantry. Harris describes existence within such a liminal zone as follows: "It is as if within his work he [the writer] sets out again and again across a certain territory of primordial, but broken, recollection in search of a species of fiction whose existence he begins to discern. By species of fiction I am thinking of a kind of intense visualization within which one is drawn or driven, to enter overlapping capacities of nature--one breaks, as it were, the spell of the self-sufficient social animal."[7] This present study, then, will focus on the interstitiality of the novels of Lamming and Harris.

Within the interstices of the plantation system, there is perhaps no more contradictory "item" than the black man. He is at once a valuable commodity and abused property, a producer of wealth and a threat to life itself. In the case of miscegenation, he is both a son and the beast of burden of his father-owner, and in the confusion between gospel bearing and ruthless plunder he is a child of God to be saved from his unenlightened ways and a creature less than human that needs to be at best protected, at worst flogged into submissive usefulness. Noble savage and dangerous rebel, he is, in a word, the ultimate ambiguity--an interstitial being. Yet potentially his worldview (antithetical to and disruptive of the dominant white social order) can infuse creative renewal into barren archaic forms.

The black slave wears ambiguous masks: Sambo and Nat Turner, warm-hearted Mammy and scheming obeah-woman. Of the last type of interstitial persons, witches, Mary Douglas says: "Here are people living in the interstices of the power structure, felt to be a threat to those with better defined status. Since they are credited with dangerous, uncontrollable powers, any excuse is given for suppressing them."[8] Thus the Negro becomes an "invisible man" at the source of power--a dangerous threat to the defined power structure that excludes him.

Although the folk are ritually excluded from the sacredness of the Great House, yet there are points at which master and slave must meet, and these meeting points are charged with sacredness and danger. Belgian anthropologist Arnold van Gennep has shown that frontiers between tribes are carefully defined, if not by a natural boundary (tree, river, sacred rock), then by some consecrated landmark: "Because of the pivoting of sacredness, the territories on either side of the neutral zone are sacred to whoever is in the zone, but the zone, in turn, is sacred for the inhabitants of the adjacent territories. Whoever passes from one to the other finds himself physically and magico-religiously in a special situation for a certain length of time: he wavers between two worlds."[9]   Potential meeting points between "worlds," van Gennep says, are crossroads and marketplaces. Indeed the "marketplace" has dominated relationships between Europe and the Third World from the beginning of a trans-Atlantic trade in human "chattel" until the present.

This symbol of the marketplace with Anancy as its presiding deity will be discussed at length in my next chapter, but one aspect of its applicability to the Caribbean writer is in the matter of publication. The contemporary marketplace experience for the Caribbean artist is the margin where Western commerce meets the creative artist's expressivity--a publisher and global distributor of his work are necessities. And since the marketplace of literary exchange (despite progress made in the establishment of publishing houses in the black world) is still ruled by publishers, universities, and big business, the artist must create and present his fictive message in such a way that the House will be persuaded to invest. Clearly, to shape a marketable fiction that exposes the rottenness of the Great House requires the artist as trickster in a very commercial sense.

The figure of trickster is universal. Lurking at crossroads, around doorways, and in public places, Trickster is god of the marketplace--Hermes in ancient Greece, Eshu-Elegba among the Yoruba, Anancy in the West Indies and the southern states of America, Wakdjunkaga among the North American Indians--and so on through culture after culture. Associated with inversion of social order, with deceit (fictions), and libido transformed into creativity, the trickster becomes a perfect image for the black artist who, confined to the margins of Europe's inscribed text, nevertheless presides, godlike, over the marketplace of linguistic exchange, signifying upon authority's text in endless wordplay and deconstruction.

In our plantation model, the trickster-artist operates on the boundary where House meets folk. But although the House-folk structure is primarily a ritual expression of colonization, colonization itself becomes a metaphor for other, subtler forms of oppression: the colonization of women by attitudes of unquestioned male supremacy, and the colonization of the mind that refuses to question its own assertions and move to greater self-knowledge. Writing in a preface to *The Whole Armour* about the conceptual polarizations that create "monsters," Harris comments, "In some degree, therefore, we need to retrieve or bring those 'monsters' back into ourselves as native to psyche, native to a quest for unity   through contrasting elements, through the ceaseless task of the creative imagination to digest and liberate contrasting spaces rather than succumb to implacable polarizations."[10] Harris adds, "Such retrieval is vision."

It is the contention of the present study that the process of recognizing "implacable polarizations" followed by a quest for unity that involves bringing "monsters" back into ourselves as native to psyche is inscribed in the fictive landscapes of both Harris and Lamming. One must attempt to first read the signs inscribed on the landscape by the colonizer and then see how the folk artist interacts with such an "authoritarian" text to deconstruct it and arrive at an alternative reading of reality--a reading that will rewrite (re-rite?) the silences and omissions of the dominant model. In such an enterprise, the folk normally become protagonists: marginalia move to center page.

It now becomes apparent that the House-folk model is rich with meaning. It appears in literal form in Lamming's *In the Castle of My Skin*, where the landlord's house and garden on the hill stand surrounded by a wall that excludes the folk whose designation is "tenantry." This tenantry, in a curiously Hegelian manner, exists only in relation to the concept "landlord." A less explicit use of the plantation model appears in *Season of Adventure*, where Eurocentricity is found in the attitudes and values of a black social elite who live on Federal Drive and operate from Federal Buildings. This elite of neocolonials is cut off from the folk whose bounded territory is the Forest Reserve. Under federation, as under the Great House of European domination, the folk are still marginalized. Yet, these marooned folk are, like the land itself (Forest), the true wealth of the nation--its reserve.[11]

In Wilson Harris's fiction, the plantation model is further abstracted. It gains a larger and more general range of signification. The Great House comes to represent unyielding authoritarian assumptions of every kind. In the polysemous method that Harris employs, preconceptions, self-image, prejudices, social structure, political or economic power are all found to be like fixed erections (the sexual pun is exploited by Harris in *Tumatumari*) that fail to impregnate and bring about renewed life. The carefully guarded ruling authority that is the historical legacy of colonization is, in Harris's terms, "incestuous"; there is a refusal of the Great House to relate to the landscape except to establish active dualities of lordship and bondage. Ruler-ruled, victor-victim, hunter-hunted, master-slave, male-female are the oft-encountered oppositions in Harris's landscapes, and such rigid dualities can only be destructive, Harris repeatedly implies. His novels aspire toward a new structuring of conceptual landscapes, for there can be no movement into new life (either on an individual or a national plane) unless, within the mutability of reality, ruling concepts repeatedly are acknowledged as limiting and then displaced by broader and more humane definitions. Master of the crossroads, the Anancy artist provokes that dialogue which brings creative disorder into the oppressive structures that dehumanize our world.

George Lamming's novels typically open on a polarized landscape: the landlord's house on the hill looks out over a tenantry below in *In the Castle of My Skin*; a ship divided between privileged officers above decks and brutalized crew below sails from Lime Stone to Black Rock in *Natives of My Person*. Typically, too, Lamming's fictions explore the boundaries within these polarized landscapes. The novel *Season of Adventure* is of particular interest in this respect since it not only establishes a polarized landscape, but also suggests a canonization of the values implicit in the dominant social structure--a suggestion that is made, one might almost say, to be unequivocally deconstructed by the central acts of the text itself.

In *Season*, a Eurocentric worldview adopted by the black neocolonial rulers of San Cristobal (Lamming's composite and paradigmatic Caribbean society shown, in this novel, during the period of the federation) has divided the island's territory into two kinds of areas, sacred and unclean ones. As Mary Douglas has demonstrated in her analysis of tribal ritual, any system of ordering necessarily involves exclusion of unwanted elements, which are thus constituted as the "dirt" or "waste" of the system. It is, however, only from resources within such excluded matter that a new system can be formed. Consequently, dirt is accorded power and is reckoned to be a danger to the existing order.[12] The folk, then, excluded as so much dirt from the social structuring of a newly independent San Cristobal, are finally revealed as a source of power. They ironically enable a false and barren society to be cleansed and made fertile. The text of *Season* thus becomes a kind of narrative rite of passage in which sterile values of the ruling black elite are transcended and the traditional folkways are reinstated as generative and renewing reserves.

A rite of passage such as I have just described is, in fact, undergone in this novel by Fola, stepdaughter of Piggott, San Cristobal's chief of police. At the invitation of Charlot, a European who taught her history at school, Fola attends a vodun Ceremony of Souls. The experience forces her to tear off the mask of social propriety that conceals her true self and launches her on a quest to find her real father, her true identity. Turning her back on the neocolonial elite to which she belongs solely by virtue of her mother's marriage to Piggott (who himself came to office by underhand means) and rejecting the tutelage of Charlot, her high-school history teacher, Fola takes as her mentor Chiki, a painter who is proletarian by birth but has been educated under the colonial system. Through Chiki her attitude to the folk changes, and her increasing involvement with the Boys of the Reserve is brought to a crisis when Chiki and his friends become chief suspects in Piggott's investigation of the murder of Raymond, vice president of the Republic. Together,

Chiki and Fola produce a picture of Fola's (imagined) father who, they imply, was the guilty party--a fiction that has the effect of incriminating the entire society, since each man identifies with the image Chiki creates. Fola's movement into the freedom of being "other than" the Fola defined by her social group is made possible only when she enters the void of ambiguity, embracing her bastard origins. Together with Fola, the entire society is confronted with the hidden "darkness" of its shadowy alter ego, its oppression of the poor and its tolerance of corruption in public officers. Just as the accusing voices of the dead challenge the composure of the living in the Ceremony, so the voices of steel drums played by the Boys of the Reserve bear testimony to the falsity and corruption of the elite. A society that has been officially declared independent and free is brought face to face with the reality of its continuing bondage to alien cultural values; its soul struggles for freedom beyond and other than that which European powers have defined. In this struggle for authentic as opposed to normal freedom, the novelist, like the houngan, is ridden by the spirit of the silenced folk, and becomes their voice in the ritual ceremony of the text.

The landscape of the text is schematically divided, as I have noted above, between Federal Buildings and Forest Reserve. Lying between these symbolic poles is a danger zone inhabited by a prison, a brothel, and a cemetery, fine symbols of the intercourse between rich and poor in San Cristobal's "marketplace." Gracious living is found on Federal Drive as in Lady Carol Baden-Semper's home, a "huge plantation house in the Maraval hills which was the finest example of colonial architecture in San Cristobal" (p. 69). The interests of black neocolonials are taken care of in Federal Buildings. Nearby, in Federal Park, immortelle trees "drip petals the color of blood" (pp. 154-155). As in the Latin *semper* (always) of Lady Carol's name, so in "immortelle" one senses the supposed enduring nature of colonial topographies. Outside the Federal buildings, though, are sweepers, blind beggars, boys "rummaging for cigarette ends," and an elderly couple. They are all strangers to the kingdom of the word; they understand nothing of the inside affairs of the system that controls their lives: "An aged couple sit together on a charitable bench in the public square and suck cooked crab backs out of an obsolete newspaper. The print dissolves in grease, taunts their reading like an absent guardian which will not let them know what happened in the federal buildings they think they dare not enter (p. 156)." In the Republic, comments the narrator ironically, "architectural relations have always been straightforward: law courts adjoin the prisons as the cemetery waits beneath the hospital windows" (p. 171).

At the boundary of this federally constructed world is the Forest Reserve. Menfolks in the Reserve are forever known as "the Boys." In contrast to the "silent columns of white marble" of Fola's home on Federal Drive with the "breath of jasmine" blowing from her garden are the mud and squalor of the yard where a black bitch chews up her offspring as they are born. Instead of the elocution lessons of the Baden-Semper's's home, the Reserve hears the obscenities of Flo, Unice, and Mathilda. Unlike the Baden-Semper's's home, the Reserve's *tonelle* boasts no piano.[13] Its music is beaten from drums whose rhythmic pulse is feared or held in contempt by the upper classes. The immortelle tree of the Reserve has "fallen into decay," and the very sky "looks like dirt" (p. 51).

In fact whatever hails from the *tonelle* is a pollutant in society's eyes. "They want to clean all what belong to behin' the times like drums an' ceremony for the dead an' all that" (p.314), explains the corporal. "Dirty ruffians the lot o' them," declares Piggott, speaking of the denizens of the Reserve. And when Aunt Jane steps out of the Reserve into Piggott's world, Therese, the Piggott's maid, is terrified of this "ol' midnight hag" (p. 111), as she calls her. We read, further, that "Therese took a step back as though she feared contamination from the old woman's touch" (p. 111). Piggott, too, only reluctantly and with dread, returns to his "black infancy" to seek "unmedical knowledge" (p. 131) as a cure for his infertility. He would prefer to forget "whorin', hunger, the whole lot" (p. 268), but his stepdaughter Fola's adventure drags him back to the "forgotten squalor of his past" (p. 306).

The polluting dirtiness of the folk as they are perceived by the Great House is suggested in the pervasive scatology of this novel. Things normally kept hidden in "polite society" are constantly displayed. As Powell and Crim, two of the Boys, make their way to the Ceremony, Powell's speech is interrupted when "wind broke like three false notes of a bugle from his behind" (p. 11). Relentlessly the narrative proceeds to describe his stopping to urinate: "A gale lifted Powell's urine over his shirt. He staggered back and clapped his hands dry. Walking towards the tree where Crim was waiting, he smelt his hands and closed his fly" (p. 13). Venereal disease is discussed at the Ceremony. A prostitute douses her consort's genitals with gin. Spitting, urination, scratching, farting, defecation are recurring events which disturb the reader just as surely as cat mess on the table disturbs Therese.

Not only is San Cristobal divided clearly between clean and dirty, sacred and profane, but the divisions are reinforced by recurring visual images of black and white. The children eat (black) licorice and (white) peppermint; vanilla ice cream and black cake are given to pacify Fola at her mother's wedding. There are white mice and black rats, white marble columns against the black sky, and white false teeth giving new identity to Piggott's caved-in black face. Eva Bartok almost betrays herself by spitting out a black thread from her black brassiere and so "desecrating" the white sink of the bathroom in the federal buildings (p. 165). Every boundary in this polarized landscape is sacralized, and everywhere purity is threatened with defilement.

A fine picture of careful framing and relentless exclusion of polluting elements is Therese's kitchen in Fola's home. Insects are mercilessly pursued, dirt is carefully cleaned away. Hence, when the household cat relieves herself on the dining-room table, the maid is so ashamed that she cleans up the mess but keeps the entire incident to herself. The stinking mess (though "natural") in the center of her (and Piggott's) carefully framed world is, like Fola's snivel in the cake and ice cream, a symbolic foreshadowing of a more dangerous "dirt" that will upset the entire social structure of San Cristobal. In her own home Therese keeps windows closed against the sound of the drums. She has imbibed the values of the "Great" to such an extent that she defines her own class and its culture as polluting. She conceals her relationship to the *tonelle* and all that it stands for. By her actions, though, she offends against nature just as surely as the mother of the boy whose soul cries out in the ceremony in quest of its origins. To deny one's "origins"--to call those origins dirt--is to be unnatural. Shame, a recurring word in *Season*, holds people back from true community. Like the woman with the boil, who appears in the first anecdote recorded in the novel, the elite of San Cristobal allow shame to deprive them of fruitful relationships.

There is danger, anthropologists tell us, in boundaries. And the danger present in the polarized world of San Cristobal is symbolized in the dominant color splashed across its black and white landscape: red.[14] The petals of immortelle trees that beautify the federal buildings and the Federal Park recall the island's violent history and anticipate the bloodshed that may accompany any transgressing of boundaries. Blood stains Raymond's scarf when the Boys meet the ruling elite as entertainers and servants at a civic function; the sky rains blood as police truncheons crunch against the bodies of the Boys; blood flows from wounds inflicted by Piggott on Fola, who to him, because of her association with the Reserve folk, is now a dangerous defilement. The bloody scene of a black bitch chewing her offspring sums up the life of San Cristobal whenever its two worlds meet.

Times, too, are changing, and the two worlds are meeting more frequently; danger is ever imminent. Under the "distinguished and hereditary planter, Sir Patrick Bloomfield" (p. 353), demarcation lines were clear. The very name Bloomfield "was sacred", and "absent and yet everywhere," he had "become like God" (p. 353). But the blooming field of the nineteenth-century plantation has given way to twentieth-century multinational corporations. Jim Aswell, owner of the local Coca Cola kingdom, may appear

altogether different, but he is an exploiter "as well." He assumes
("Jim as well") an informal stance, and his democratic methods
certainly reflect the results of the Labor movement celebrated by
Chiki on the occasion of the British prime minister's visit, yet,
despite Aswell's camaraderie, danger lingers in the meeting of
capital owner and worker. Employee Kem Barrett feels the need
to keep certain "standards" in his dress and is conscious of
"shame" in Aswell's presence. Both words have an accumulated
negative charge in the novel.   Aswell realizes that Barrett's
political activism, though no threat where the police are concerned, "would certainly disturb the work in his factories for
three or four days. And there was nothing Aswell valued more
deeply than time" (p. 355). Any disruption of the money-making
process has to be dealt with summarily; the interests of San
Cristobal are subordinate to those of multinational corporations.
Jim Aswell is merely another "arse-hole" through which authority
relieves itself. In this particular instance, Aswell's action helps
the local cause, but the shadow of corporate industry looms like
Sir Patrick's Great House over the San Cristobal landscape.

Within the topography created by capitalism, the worker is
reified, and the purely utilitarian character of human relationships within the commercial nexus is echoed in the pervasive
references to prostitution. Money ruins Gort's relationship with
Bobby Chalk, the blind Englishman who had formerly been so
close to the folk that he had been renamed Old Magdala and
initiated into the secret codes of the bands.   Exploitative
economic relationships destroy all the bonds of love, loyalty, and
kinship.

Danger threatens, but few are aware. Seeing only immortelles,
and blind to blood, the polite society of San Cristobal (paradigmatic of privilege at international levels) considers itself clean,
undefiled, and authoritative. Lamming, however, in a series of
subtle inversions, shifts from the notion of cleanliness to that of
sterility to show that barrenness and not purity characterizes this
privileged group. The vibrant sexuality of Eva, who hails from
the street of brothels, Bruton Lane, stands in sharp contrast to the
onanistic premarital activities of Squires and Veronica, an-
ticipated in Veronica's masturbatory custom of taking food and
sweets to bed where she "relished the feeling of eating alone
unseen" (p. 68). While the *tonelle* is alive with the voices of
children, Doctor Camillon, faced in the maternity hospital with
a case of abortion, is satisfied to "let it rot in her guts"--even
when the woman concerned is Eva, mother of his own unborn
and, of course, unacknowledged child. Piggott, whatever posture
he assumes to do "that fertilizing and decisive it" (p. 129), and
however hard he sweats at the project, is impotent to impregnate
his wife, Agnes. "Somewhere *beyond this house* there is a reservoir
of water; sea and river are ever generous in their gifts," he

ponders, yet for him "the taps are still, barren" (p. 128, emphasis mine). The restraints polite society imposes are unnatural. They are as false as the teeth Piggott wears to hide the crumpled face that the public must not see. In Veronica's thoughts, the worst thing that could happen to Fola would be "it"--pregnancy consequent on the "rape" by one of the Boys. Yet in Eva's eyes, sexuality and pregnancy are a matter for delight, not shame. What to Eva's mind is shameful is the so-called virtuous restraint of people like Veronica. While sweepers outside ensure the clean appearance of Federal Buildings, Eva, inside this sacred place, exposes the hidden filth of society when she levels her accusation against Veronica and Fola: "You can play great ... you can walk like your heel on hot ash, can't open your crutch for fear your pride leak out. But below where everything hide, you not only like anybody else, you so and different 'cause you nasty, the two of you, plain, stinking nasty" (p. 169).

Such anxiety as the ruling class of San Cristobal shows over sexual defilement from contact with the folk is an expression of that class's insecurity, for "desire" that reaches across boundaries implies ontological equality. Mary Douglas suggests that "when rituals express anxiety about the body's orifices the sociological counterpart of this anxiety is a care to protect the political and cultural unity of a minority group."[15] Through his use of pollution concepts, Lamming implies that a rigid caste structure constitutes the dominant mental landscape of the neocolonial ruling class of San Cristobal.

In the first half of *Season*, which is narrated from Fola's initial point of view inside the dominant social structure, dirt and corruption attach to the folk. From her conceptual frame, her "window"--the "hole from which she watched the world" (p. 84)--she sees other children as "dirty black rats." But by the time Fola's rite of passage is over she sees clearly that the center of corruption is, in fact, in the self-styled high priests of social standards. In the novel's second half, from her new vantage point outside society and in the company of the black artist Chiki and the women of Moon Glow bar, she links the Ceremony of Souls with the "dead" in society--those who, like Baden-Semper, are tied to the past, but are unable to leap beyond history into a freely chosen future: "She had begun to realize what was the ultimate punishment of the dead. She thought she saw the limitation in each corpse which had returned to tell its history. It was this obvious and overwhelming fact: they had no future they could choose. Memory was their last and only privilege. They could not leap beyond themselves, beyond the moment their own story had ended" (pp. 246-247). Fola comes to see that the Reserve's criminals and prostitutes may not be society's real dirt. Society's "pollution" comes to appear as her own social group. Her class of neocolonials are "the decrepit skeletons near the

Federal Drive, polluting the live air with wave upon wave of their corpse breathing" (p. 247). Their spending is a "contagion" (p. 245); their social intercourse is nothing but a "man-fabricated tomb of getting together when words come plentiful as dirt" (p. 124). As the dirt of corruption in high places is exposed through Chiki's fiction, a plague of sandflies blows in clouds over San Cristobal.

Pollution at the very center of sacredness sums up much of the imagery of *Season*: donkey dung in the sanctuary, and catmess on the dining table. Fola's resolve to "wage her war in the sanctuary of the Maraval hills and in the sacred residences which freedom had lately named Federal Drive" (p. 245) is a trespassing of boundaries. It exposes the ritually cleansed temples as the breeding ground of all of San Cristobal's putrefaction and contamination. The woman of Powell's story who *appeared* to be virtuously resisting premarital sexual overtures was, in fact, only afraid to confess to having a boil on her bottom. Society's frenetic concern with "standards"--by which is meant imported standards, not standards natural to the folk--is a desperate attempt to conceal its own rottenness.

Within the "defiled" world that stands *pro fana*--outside the sacred structure with its idols of money, correct deportment, classical music, good grammar, and valuable connections--there is an alternative center of sacredness: the *tonelle*. This meticulously inscribed landscape is described in detail by Lamming:

> The tonelle was an ordinary meeting place, a clean perimeter of earth partitioned by the night. The pole rose from the center of the yard, climbing through seven feet of shaven joints, dry as bone, to make a funnel through the ceiling: this was the mythical stairs down which the invisible gods would soon descend. A thick, white line of maize marked a circle round the pole, leaving an area of ground untouched by the women who danced around it. No one could trespass within the circle until the gods had arrived. (pp. 21-22)

Turning their backs on the false gods that live on Federal Drive, the folk of the Reserve await the arrival of other gods--their own, not an imposed heritage of ideals and values. The folk ritual has totally reversed the clean/dirty constructs of the dominant culture, locating purity in the very heart of the *tonelle*. The sanctity of the central pole of "mythical stairs" is indicated by the "clean perimeter of earth" and the "white line of maize." The only partition is where the edges of the light thrown by the flambeaux meet the darkness of night in which the ruling class is sleeping, oblivious of the rhythms that pulse with life in the rejected shanty town of the Reserve. Boundaries in this landscape suggest not exclusion but an invitation to inclusion. It is essentially a meeting place; the central "stairway," the "bridge" of prostrate women, and the "corridors" of dust create a landscape of communication channels between living and dead, gods and men. Where the western mode adopted by the upper classes is an ideological system of stratification and division, the *tonelle* removes these structural features, taking us into a liminal region where the insignia of western status are not applicable. Even Charlot, Fola's English history teacher, may be present, though only as a spectator; the houngan reveals the sacra in this learning experience. Fola, child of privilege in her own society, becomes a child indeed in the ceremony, while Liza--one of the "black rats"--dances with complete assurance.

An impulse to inclusiveness and integration is similarly evident in the arrangement of the sacra of the *houngan*'s "sanctuary": "The African goddess, Erzulie, resided in the left alcove. She stared across a cubicle of space at a picture of the Virgin Mary on the other side. The saints of Congo and Senegal were observing them from the far corner of the room" (p. 43).

Paradox and contradiction (major aspects of liminality) figure in the "easy alliance" of the African gods with the Virgin Mary, as in the fact that the *houngan* will attend mass at the Roman Catholic church on the morrow of the ceremony. The folk have adjusted the boundaries defining their world in a creative response to a dual (bastard) heritage. Charlot reacts in naive romanticism to the creolization process: "Like the poetry of his own language their faith was, perhaps, a ground of being which balanced every variation of belief" (p. 41). There is truth in Charlot's statement. But he fails to see the subtle implications of the *houngan*'s ambiguous arrangement. The positioning of Erzulie, goddess of love, and the Virgin Mary as "comfortable neighbors" not only takes from Christianity its privileged status, but also, because of its context of saints' names, comments scathingly on the self-styled pure "virgins" like Veronica who, despite their protestations, are in no way superior to the Eva Bartoks or the Belindas who side with Erzulie. In fact, "read" in this way, the nonverbal signifying of oral tradition volubly denies any privileged status or sacredness to the imposed culture. Where it appears to honor, it is really doing just the opposite. The omnipresent trickster figure of folk tradition has been busy introducing ambiguity right here in the *tonelle*!

Charlot's response to the Ceremony is that of an outsider. He is European. He approaches the Ceremony's mystery with a western perceptual frame--describing, explaining, analyzing, when he is required to experience at a level other than the rational and logical. Thus he studies, but never fully understands. As Liza says, Charlot keeps "in the light all the time, but his face still don't come clear" (p. 57). His statement that the ververs are "the source of all the visual arts in San Cristobal" (p.

25) is true, yet in a far deeper sense than he has begun to suspect. For him it is "not every niggling detail, but the *large* events" (p. 28) of history that matter, while the very message of the *tonelle* is that events in time that we call facts are mere fictions. The reality lies somewhere between and behind the acts, and it is not structure and status that matter but relationships. Lamming's own concern to communicate not the facts but the inner meaning of the Ceremony is mirrored in Chiki's frustration as he tries to make sketches of the dances: "It ain't enough to understand what they are doing, and ain't enough to change it either" (p. 49), he says to Charlot, then tears up his sketches.

Chiki's angry words and his desire to put the ancient rituals into a new form of communication are revealing. Indeed, the tension between the oral and the written informs all of Lamming's work. When the *houngan* acknowledges Charlot, the English history teacher, as his "brother from afar" (p. 45), he points up the inextricable ties between European history and the exploited folk of the Caribbean, between the text and its silences. Similarly, the music of Jack o' Lantern's resurrected drum and songs of the folk stand over against the authority of the word: Baako's speech over the radio and the power of his signature appended to documents in the national parliament (p. 361). Indeed, the struggle between the voice of the people (imaged in the souls of the Ceremony, the drums, and the songs) and the written *word* of authority (imaged in the laws that seek to "wipe out" the drums and all that they represent), is early set out in Crim's recollection of Jack o' Lantern's words to the judge who sentenced him to death: "Your Honour, I don't care who make the country's laws if they let me make the country's music" (p. 20). When, in response to Baako's speech, Gort plays "Lead, Kindly Light" on his drum, it is no Christian sentiment, but an invocation of the spirit of Jack o' *Lantern* himself: an oral heritage takes precedence over received texts.

Just as the *houngan* stands between the living and the dead, and just as Chiki seeks to spatialize an aural/oral experience in his art, so the Caribbean novelist stands in a no man's land between the text and oral tradition. He combines, as it were, both historian and *houngan*, and yet is neither of these. When Chiki tears up his sketches of an African heritage in the Caribbean, he points to the inadequacy of mimesis, of realism, as a means of communicating folk experience. A mere recovery and representation will no more heal San Cristobal than will the elite's clutching at historical ties with Europe--mockingly imaged in Piggott's youthful attempts to be a "real soldier" exactly like the photograph of Colonel Carlysle (p. 121). To rewrite history is not enough; to mirror colonial education, the Labor movement, Federation, emigration, Independence--even though from a Caribbean perspective--is to miss the real rhythms of folk life.

Between these epic structures resounds the music of the drums--vibrant and vital, though not inscribed in any official text.

Lamming's solution is to use language so ambiguously that his text deconstructs itself as it proceeds. The reader, for instance, is tempted to side with San Cristobal's elite in accounting the Ceremony as unclean when he reads that decay surrounds the *houngan* and that "the smell of cemeteries rotted his hands" (p. 32). But the odor of decay that lingers around the houngan, concerned as he is to give a voice to the past that authority wishes to silence, is not to be compared with the corruption of authority itself. For Piggott and his deputy, Lady Carol, her husband, and Raymond, all have grown wealthy and gained political power by means of forged currency made by one Guru, whose spirit is summoned in the Ceremony. Small wonder that voices are silenced by law when the makers of the law have such secrets to hide. Lamming's art is to discover the past, to re-member the broken god, but in so doing to lay bare the arbitrary connections that make for epic, and to reveal a vital counter-movement, an energeia, in the word-less signifying of the folk.

Since his work is anti-epic, it is the folk, not an individual, who, corporately, are the hero. Individuals in Lamming's fiction are always flawed, and their perceptions are always partial. Although Chiki, for instance, is mentor to Fola, and although his work produces the revolutionary upheaval in San Cristobal, the artist is blinded with prejudice against the upper classes and has, in fact, lost touch with the folk. His refusal to visit Aunt Jane in hospital and his final despair both mark him as a flawed person. Lamming denies us any hero or any permanently valid point of view. Indeed, the novel's exposure of our limited perceptual frame argues implicitly for a plurality of discourse. In his hands, the Haitian vodun Ceremony thus becomes a basic metaphor for the need to move repeatedly from structured premises into antistructure in order to reassess the validity of accepted norms.

The Ceremony, then, stands antithetically over against the values of the San Cristobal elite. The empiricism, materialism, and individualism of the westernized class expressed through the "architecture" of the landscape centered on Federal Buildings find no place in the *tonelle*. Here all structures are impermanent. Maize seeds form shapes that will be broken up as the Ceremony proceeds, and the *houngan*'s hut is about to collapse. Both are expressive of flux. All that is rejected in the world of Federal Drive is given prominence in the Reserve. Nature, instinct, trance, ecstatic utterance--in a word the realm of the unconscious--are preeminent in the Reserve. The *tonelle* is antistructure; it is the underside of society (if we read the novel as social criticism) and the underside of the psyche (if we read the narrative as a self-reflexive commentary on the process of creativity itself.)

To move, as Fola does, outside of the "House" of our certainties, challenging our "premises" and "structures," whether social or conceptual, in an embrace of the unknown and untried, is to experience a kind of dying. It is such a death that Fola embarks on when she rejects the false identity she has been given and searches for her true paternity. Chiki's message is that there must be a backward glance, and only a glance, and then a leap beyond that fixed, inscribed self into a future where one is "other than" the identity imposed by others, "beyond" the name that another has called us by. Significantly it is under Chiki's tutelage, not Charlot's, that Fola makes her dying into a new existence as the tomb/womb paradox of the *tonelle* is realized in her experience. For Fola makes her own rite of passage in *Season*. Physically, she moves beyond the boundaries of the circumscribed world into the public ward of the hospital and the brothel and returns to her Federal Drive home as a pollutant, a dangerous liminal figure whom Piggott has to expel from his sanctuary. In ritual she goes to the *tonelle*, shares communion with the folk, enters the tomb/womb of the houngan's hut, and identifies with Liza during her "fearful encounter with her forgotten self" (p. 50). But at a deeper metaphysical level, Fola moves into an interstructural space where her meditation on her past becomes a meditation on the very nature of the structuring process, on consciousness itself. During the liminal period, says Victor Turner, "neophytes are alternately forced and encouraged to think about their society, their cosmos, and the powers that generate and sustain them. Liminality may be partly described as a stage of reflection."[16] "Reflection" in the present discussion suggests contemplating the process of consciousness itself. Fola's ritual movement into the liminal sphere is symbolized by geographical displacement, disguise, and association with death, unconsciousness, and solitude.[17] We find her "alone and in the disguise of a boy" (p. 65) on the "outskirts" of the Reserve. Ill and slightly delirious with fever, she stands between consciousness and unconsciousness--a condition reflected in her physical situation among the graves of the Sargasso cemetery where she hovers between life and death. Back in her bedroom, her ritual liminality symbolically established, she embarks on an examination of the structuring of her life, as it appears in the framed photographs of her past.

The photographs in their frames are, like Charlot's history, an attempt at accurate or realistic representation--an authoritative record: "Fola's past was framed upon these walls" (p. 68). But Fola is no longer seduced by the pictures. First she drops the picture of Charlot, breaking the frame. Next she examines the photograph of Therese. The servant's "small dark eyes betrayed no hint of her cunning," Fola remarks, and as Fola reminisces on an incident that had revealed Therese's nature she can now see the arrogance and cunning in the servant's face with "the chin tilted at an angle above her mother's shoulder" (p. 66). The camera, for all its pretended objectivity, is limited to a particular angle, a circumscribing frame. Each ideologically framed "history" is challenged by its silenced omissions.

As Fola shifts her attention from the subjects of the pictures to their "frame"--that is, to the perceptual prefiguration that has set them off for privileged consideration--she begins to see the system of ordering the world that is peculiar to the education she has received. Fola meditates, too, on the "improbable journey across that dark margin of space between ... photographs" (p. 68). It is the link between episodes that now captures her--the omissions of the text and its unspoken assumptions. Rejecting Charlot's method of discounting the "niggling detail" in one's pursuit of the "large events," she is now preoccupied with the interstices, the silences of the record, with another world "beyond the pictures on the wall," and "beyond Charlot's scrutiny" (p. 75). Memory now supplies Fola with that liminal reading of the past, and, where memory fails, questions. She realizes, too, that mutability, not fixity, is the nature of things: "These different worlds of time changed without warning, changing their own emphasis of meaning. The light made an edge of shadow that reached to the broken frame of memories from Mourant Bay" (p. 69). Every new "reading" of the past, every reflection on the fact, shifts its meaning, constantly creating anew what Charlot would consider a fixed monument. The world of Charlot's people is made permanent, established, in the "architecture of their history," and responses to their monuments are "determined by their sense of expectation, as though they had chosen without evidence to be wholly identified with what was not yet known" (p. 73). Fola's new understanding tells her that such fixity is a falsification; the elapse of time produces subtle changes in meaning so that viewing the past from the standpoint of the present inevitably distorts that reality. Similarly for Americans in search of monuments, recorded history presents no problems because the record is "wholly contained in their own way of looking at the world" (p. 93). But from Fola's point of view, history was a "commercial deportation," a saga of disruption and discontinuity. "All vision was balanced on that difference between herself and Charlot" (p. 93). Charlot's past is an edifice, a monument; Fola's is an absence, a silence.

Hayden White, in refutation of the assumed objectivity of historical method, points to the opacity of language itself, which makes every discourse tend toward metadiscursive reflexiveness. White argues that "all original descriptions of any field of phenomena are already interpretations of its structure, and ...

the linguistic mode in which the original description (or taxonomy) of the field is cast will implicitly rule out certain modes of representation and modes of explanation regarding the field's structure and tacitly sanction others."[18] Having established that techniques of emplotment, description, and analysis assume a peculiar posture in the face of reality, that the words in which we encode reality are themselves opaque, and that "all language is politically contaminated," White explains that "it is not a matter of choosing between objectivity and distortion, but rather between different strategies for constituting 'reality' in thought so as to deal with it in different ways each of which has its own ethical implications."[19] Thus, although mimesis is imprisoned in language, and although every discourse apparently and inevitably prefigures and preconstitutes, it is possible for the speaker to be both conscious and critical of the mode of prefiguration he is using: "The structure of any sophisticated, i.e., self-conscious and self-critical discourse, mirrors or replicates the phases through which consciousness itself must pass in its progress from a naive (metaphorical) to self-critical (ironic) comprehension of itself."[20]

What White writes of the French philosopher Michel Foucault is eminently true of Fola. Like Foucault's, her method is to ignore "continuities, traditions, influences, causes, comparisons, typologies," and to examine "ruptures," "discontinuities," and "disjunctions."[21] Like Foucault, as well, Fola "celebrates the spirit of creative *dis*ordering, *de*structuration, *un*naming."[22] Her deconstructive movement from appreciation of fixed record to an ironic appraisal of the mode of its constitution seen in her moments with the photographs is at once her means of access to freedom from the domination of the text and a key to her creator's literary technique. As she lies in bed, we read that "the mirror begged her to stare, but the light couldn't climb beyond its shadow on the wall. Yet the night like a surface of black glass reflected a crowd of faces that were not there" (p. 94). The photographs symbolized a constituting prefiguration of reality that distorts and falsifies both by the camera's point of view and by its omissions. The mirror, too, now fails Fola: her true self is not to be seen in the reflection of her face as it is now, for she contains all her past, all her relationships, all her experience. And so she turns to the blackness for her light: to memory, to imagination--to the "surface of black glass" reflecting her forgotten self.

Fola now has seen the limitations of Charlot's worldview: the angle of perception, the limited frame, the omissions and arbitrary connections, and the failure to come to terms with change. Yet, for all her insight, she cannot be totally free of the "architecture" of his history. Her "death," as she lies in her bed "no wider than a grave," hears again the drums of the *tonelle*, and feels for herself the waters imprisoning the souls in the

Ceremony, takes her into a liminality where the paradox of her dual world is resolved. Again, it is the nonrational that is celebrated--the insight of dream: "Like the ceremony of souls, her dream was making a harmony of moments at once familiar and improbable. It had combined two different worlds; yet they were real, beyond any logic of contradiction in her mind" (p. 95). In vision, Fola sees Lady Carol, Veronica, and Agnes enter the tonelle in confrontation with the truth about themselves. Only then does the island rise out of its baptism of fire, wind, and water to be reborn: "Soon the flambeaux had split wide open. The island rose like a turtle from its sloth, entirely cuddled in flames, blossoming a weather that cleansed its crust with water and fire. The floods were ready to swallow her up, and every house, hurricane risen to the moon, now sailed in a mad division of roof and walls over the nearest tide" (pp. 95-96). Floods, hurricane, fire, tide--all features of West Indian experience, and all implying destruction of boundaries--point to a natural yet violent period of change, mirrored throughout the novel in a sky giving bloody birth to the new moon: "The new moon was thrusting up through little clots of blood which mottled half of the old moon's face" (p. 243).

Fola's "season of adventure" in her deconstruction of the photographs in her life begins with her discovery of the silences, the interstices of the "text" that she has accepted hitherto. She will now step outside of its frame, demonstrating that she is Fola and "other than" Fola, and in so doing will claim for herself a creative future denied to those who remain fixed in the text of another's authorship. Her rite of passage, which has blurred the boundary between history and memory, the articulated and the silent, leads to the next phase of our discussion: the drums and the inarticulate folk. For the Ceremony and the drums, together, are the voice of the folk, the sole memory of the silences in the "text." As Crim says, "education wipe out everythin' San Cristobal got except the ceremony an' the bands" (p. 17).

San Cristobal's rulers, following the example of their former colonizers, have given primacy to the written word, to formal western education and "authoritative" texts. They also adhere devoutly to a received religion that designates African religious tradition as black magic. To be in possession of the word is to be in a position of power: Carol Baden-Semper's triumph over her stammer and the social authority she gains by being able to teach elocution find their inverse image in her husband who, "imitating the pompous fluency" of his wife's speech, stuns the guests at their wedding anniversary dinner by offering to "aporkiate" the roast pork (p. 157). This likable, self-taught man, whose lively wit, Fola ponders, "had warmth and a certain sea roughness," is humiliated, driven to be "silent in his own home" (p. 80), and his marriage ruined because of Lady Carol's acceptance of the primacy of "correct" speech. The same attitude is repeated at a lower social level in Eva's mockery of her sister (p. 157).

In San Cristobal, words, fluently used, are signifiers, not of meaning, but of social worth and authority. Lady Carol instructs all the "college caste" in elocution, the "course she emphasized in her curriculum for gracious living" (p. 69). Language has thus become a means of veiling rather than revealing. This fact is supremely evident in the ambiguities in speeches made by Dr. Baako, who has taken Raymond's place as the republic's new president. Baako, in "the most arrogant speech the radio has ever allowed," uses eloquence to veil his lack of popular support and his tendency toward dictatorship. Gort follows the speech with a solo on Jack o' Lantern's resurrected drum, ironically choosing the hymn "Lead, Kindly Light, amid the encircling gloom" for the occasion, and the narrator comments, "The night was dark, but no one seemed to notice the contrast between this home and the harbour in which Jack o' Lantern had not long arrived" (p. 364). Baako, with his perception that language is at the heart of the nation's problem and that there is need for a "language which was no less immediate than the language of the drums" (p.2 63) is at once speaking the truth and revealing how dangerous he is. For his words may well be a mere means of manipulation--particularly as the narrator links him with Lady Carol: "Like Lady Carol and her phrase about the First World War, Kofi James-Williams Baako would end every public lecture by saying that the universities in a post-colonial country could serve no purpose unless they deserted the ancient notions of an elite" (p. 322). The sentiment is fine, but how much sincerity is there? In concealing a heart of darkness within a Kurtz-like grandiloquence, Baako is following the European tradition as Charlot had earlier described it: "Time and the skill of poets had forged their language into the finest instrument of speech he could imagine. One word to release an image that returned your meaning perfectly balanced by an infinity of lucid shades. Without this grace of language given, the corpse might have been betrayed" (p. 37).

The folk, on the other hand, are outside the kingdom of the word. Writing is a mystery to Gort. Speeches, newspapers, books, proclamations, lectures, and education are the property of the oppressors; stammering, dumbness, and shamefaced silence are properties of the folk. Elocution and eloquence are two quite different things, though. Nonverbal signifying is represented as *signally* eloquent in *Season*. The ververs, the arrangement of the *houngan*'s tent, Gort's refusal to eat sugar, Ashton's coffin anchored to his hair, Crim's venomous fast bowling at cricket all "speak" volubly. The sandflies that plague the island are "dumb yet eloquent as the voice of God" (p. 333), and, supremely, the drums speak to the island with "dumb eloquence" (p. 93). For

Gort, the drum is his voice: "his hands had taught that steel to talk" (p. 289). San Cristobal's "inarticulate" masses are like the souls in the *tonelle*, crying out for justice. And, as in the *tonelle*, so in the republic, it is the drums that speak for the people. The unity and release experienced by the people as the drums beat out the calypsos and digging songs, songs of the folk and hymns of the chapel, are expressed in a supremely lyrical passage. Children join in, seizing frying pans and an old woman's chamber pot as instruments: this is the people's music--their creative response to the fragmentation of experienced reality.

Scatology that attached to the folk at the novel's beginning now is ironically inverted and folk life is revealed as far other than the "dirt" of neocolonial conception. Now that the folk have found a voice in their music, a transformation occurs. "Kettles soon lost their criminal face of soot as the spoons scraped them clean with sound" (p. 359), and the chamber pot symbolically becomes the vessel of creative life. As the owner of the pot laughingly deposits her urine over the tree roots, her gesture signals the paradoxical life-giving power of what one particular system has defined as waste.

Trash is transformed into pulsing life-rhythms as the islanders create carnival. Economic and political oppression may have all but destroyed or buried the sacred ceremonial drum of African heritage, as surely as Jack o' Lantern's drum lies buried and Gort's is destroyed by the police, but out of the "waste" of neocolonialism, new drums sing out the old life-affirming rhythms. Music beaten from trash cans symbolizes the triumph of black creativity over oppression: "a simple myth of man's invention transformed by the music of his hands into the miracle of Cana's wine" (p. 361). For the drums give shape to the unrecorded past of the folk, resurrecting the buried, silent folk heritage and transmuting generations of suffering into a voice. The triumph of the drums is their ability to give new life to old forms--to turn water into wine. Under the magic of the drums the folk had seen "the *tonelle* transformed into a real, familiar tomb; and the corpses like Lazarus climbed back to life, denying the power and the permanence of the grave. That hymn had been learnt from a foreign tongue; but it had found cradle in the rhythm of the drums which were always there" (p. 360). Recontextualized by the art of music, the past of the folk is miraculously reborn from the "cradle" of the drum not as shame or suffering, but as the "wine" of triumphant celebration.

Yet the triumph is short-lived, for the new President, Baako, has a hearing problem, and the drums can speak only to those who can hear. The need still remains for a mediator, an edgeman standing between the oral tradition of the drums and the world of those who are "deaf" and so depend on the written word. The banner that Chiki designs and the cards he and Fola write are necessary supplements to Gort's efforts if the revolution is to succeed. Merely to "resurrect" Jack o' Lantern's drum (symbolizing revival of an Afro-Caribbean heritage) will not effect the creative social change Lamming envisions. For innovation lies not in extant structures, but at the junctures where these structures meet. Paradoxically, the pulsing rhythms of folk life must be stilled, frozen on the page, so that they can be communicated to a world that cannot hear. There must be a "death" as the uttered word becomes the word "locked in space," and direct experience is mediated through the falsifying forms of fiction.[23] Reality is endlessly recontextualized. The artist's tragedy (exemplified in Chiki's frustration) is that he knows he must devitalize in order to immortalize.

The Caribbean artist is an edgeman in another sense, too. In holding a mirror up to his world, the writer straddles the boundary where art and politics meet. In the tradition of calypso, the bands, masquerade, storytelling and carnival, the truly West Indian novel is a parodic response to extant forms. In keeping close to contemporary West Indian life, Lamming's novels perennially explore the art/politics boundary. In *Season*, the narrator intrudes in his own voice, accepting responsibility for Powell's violence, claiming Powell as his brother. This merging of real with fictive counterpoints the "fiction" of Chiki's portrait affecting events in the "real" world of Piggott and Raymond. Such blurring of the margin between fictive and real invites consideration of the role of the artist in society. Lamming's reply to political questions he implicitly raises lies in his shaman-trickster portrayal of the artist (to be discussed later). Chiki rejects the revolutionary stance of Powell but sells his paintings to Baako, making his vision available to the political leadership--presumably with the same mocking aplomb with which he sold Jordan water in Virginia! He insists on the potential for change born of the vitality of the folk. As possessor of the word, he straddles the boundary of orality and literacy, voicing the protest of the inarticulate. Maker of "images," he challenges the false gods of society. The artist--inhabitant of the margins--is the expiatory figure of the tribe, handling the "dangerous" material that society prefers to ignore, insisting on a reexamination of the framing principles that determine what shall be deemed holy and what defiles. The *houngan* of the Ceremony yields, in a changing society, to the artist, who leads his public through the fictive void of uncertainty and change into a vision of a new order.

His trade with the ambiguities of the word makes Chiki a stranger to the folk, his antithetical stance alienates him from the ruling class, and his refusal to be limited to any narrow, one-sided perspective leads the revolutionary, Powell, to discount Chiki as a dreamer who has betrayed the cause. The artist is, therefore, the universally rejected and marginalized expiatory sacrifice. But beyond all this he is torn within himself--divided to the vein, as Walcott has seen--over the paradox of language itself.[24] And with this we come to the major ambivalence of this novel. Lamming, as writer, recognizes that the words he uses in his fiction are the only means of communicating with a world dominated by the written word. As Mircea Eliade has pointed out, " The revolution brought about by writing was irreversible. Henceforth the history of culture will consider only archaeological documents and written texts. A people without this kind of documents is considered a people without history .... To interest a modern man ... oral traditional heritage has to be presented in the form of a book."[25] But that same written form necessary to provide historicity in the sense Eliade speaks of fails to capture the rhythms of the drums--the very rhythms of life in San Cristobal. Laming's quarrel with language is at the heart of twentieth-century thought, for we are constituted in language, yet the silences beyond the "prison-house" of language are always there, struggling for expression. The souls in the Ceremony, helpless in their inarticulate state, represent every man and woman in the castle of their skin, signified upon, but never truly mirrored by the language that alone offers hope of release. Lamming's reading of *The Tempest* and Prospero's gift to Caliban of language takes on a metaphysical dimension as Caliban becomes a metaphor for the human soul colonized by the word.[26]

Wilson Harris's intense involvement with landscape in his writing is immediately evident. Forests and rivers, waterfalls and caves, ruins and petroglyphs, animal life and flora--all are invested with symbolic energy in his novels. Our specific interest here, though, is with his establishment of a plantation model that will be reversed as his narrative proceeds. In several novels Harris uses the heartland/coastland opposition--particularly rich in connotation for a country geographically facing Europe from its narrow, cultivated (masklike) coastal strip, yet facing inland across vast regions of uncharted terrain, full of potential wealth and danger in its southward visage toward an antithetical continent. Given such a radically varied topography, the concept of arbitrary boundaries imposed by generations of conquerors is, logically, a perennial theme.

In more recent novels by Harris, in which the narrating persona is situated in Europe, the fictive patterns change, but only superficially. The surface/depth, mask/face oppositions remain. Constantly the model is of a surface-imposed structure, which we have chosen to describe as the Great House, and the concealed darkness--that terrain beyond the plantation, untamed, full of threat, yet paradoxically rich in resources. A final common denominator in all of Harris's novels is the inevitable presence of gargantuan forces that threaten boundaries. Flood and erosion, eclipse and tidal movement, death and decay--these and other phenomena become symbolic forces charged with meaning in the psyche's hinterland. The empoldered plantation thus signifies human efforts to impose ordered structure on a chaotic experience of reality.

The landscape of *The Whole Armour* (1962), Harris's third novel and part of his Guiana Quartet, is one of threatened boundaries. Abram, a solitary recluse with whom the novel begins, lives on the very edge of society--a liminal position reflected in the description of his hut: " He had built a parody of a hut on a spit of land that looked unyielding and hard amidst the trenches until they were crowded with a gnarled husk and mask and a twisted alphabet of timber. Every private notice and fable and boundary against the sea stood in the turmoil of the foreshore as in a graveyard of sculptured history and misadventure" (p. 17). Man's longing is for a space "unyielding and hard" and an enduring "sculptured history" (the adjective "sculptured" is a leitmotif in the novel) but nature denies him this. Instead, the curiously signifying landscape of "twisted alphabet" is one familiar with mutability, its "crumbling foreshore" battered repeatedly as it is by the surf: "Behind their backs the waves had begun to quake and leap in all directions and the subdued subterranean roar of the vital repression of the surf began to invade their stranded senses. Jigsaw Bay always mounted this late sudden tidal reaction: the bay would grow violent and treacherous with the new erosive impact of the sullen seas where not long before had been seeming high ground" (p. 34).

With the clause "the vital repression of the surf began to invade their stranded senses," we find ourselves in yet another dimension of liminality: between the realistic description of a geographical landscape and the metaphoric topography of the psyche. Immediately we recognize the technique of the myth-maker. Myth, according to Roland Barthes, is "a peculiar system in that it is constructed from a semiological chain which existed before it; it is a second-order semiological system. That which is a sign (namely the associative total of a concept and an image) in the first system, becomes a mere signifier in the second."[27] Thus "repression of the surf" as a sign having one meaning within the system of literal description becomes, when we accept the Jungian overtones, a signifier within the second-order system-- that of the turbulence experienced within the divided psyche. Yet there is a constant crossing and recrossing of the sign/signifier boundary within Harris's work; the reader must hold both literal and metaphoric readings simultaneously, privileging neither synchronic nor diachronic in the effort to establish meaning.

Certainly Harris's writing betrays an intense concern with the word, but for the purpose of this chapter we will put aside the semiological aspect and consider liminality within the landscape more in its mythic character as a reflection of the psyche, and the novel as a Guyanese perspective on Jung's notion of the "marriage of opposites" as prerequisite to wholeness.

Our apprehension of Harris as mythmaker will confine itself, then, to his attempts to find in the local landscape an objective correlative for the psyche of his people. The liminality of his landscape will be examined as the sacred zone in which myths of origins are retold. Abram's hut, for example, is not the only dwelling that is built in a no-man's-land. The village itself, in the riverain Pomeroon district, is "an enormous half-world and half-shadow composed of empoldered plantations and a veneer of settlement against the encroachment of the sea and the river and--above all--the jungle" (p. 49). And on a larger, continental scale, we see national boundaries threatened by the prowling tiger: "The visitation of the tiger was a feature that accompanied everyone's growing years, descending from the headwaters of the Venezuelan Cuyuni across the jungled Guiana watershed into the half-settled Pomeroon, prowling always on the frontier between changing fantasy and the growth of a new settlement" (p. 37). On every hand man constructs boundaries; on every hand his fragile constructs of civilization are threatened by forces he fears and cannot control. Or, to return to our model image, man constructs his Great House, but beyond its boundaries lurk monsters that threaten every certainty.

Anthropologist Mary Douglas, speaking of man's need to order his environment, to make his world "conform to an idea," finds in the purification rituals of various societies an expression of that idea. Ordering of the "landscape"--whether of the terrain, the family dwelling, or a meal--has to do with communicating a sense of order. Douglas, thus, believes that "ideas about separating, purifying, demarcating and punishing transgressions have as their main function to impose system on an inherently untidy experience. It is only by exaggerating the difference between within and without, above and below, male and female, with and against, that a semblance of order is created."[28] My contention is that the "idea" that orders the landscape of the village community in The Whole Armour is identical to the colonial topography of the plantation and its Great House: in other words, that the Guyanese psyche remains colonized even though the nation is technically independent. Harris, however, sets over and against the plantation's polarizations the possibility of a new world conception that will shatter cherished constructs of an old world and bring forth from a union of opposites (landlord/slave, tyrant/folk, present/past, word/silence) a future liberated from the shadow of tyrannical imposed authority.

The authority of the White House is affirmed and upheld only by means of the marginalization of the shadow half-world of blackness and the employment of black people as composite scapegoat--the eternal negative of the assumed rightness of whiteness. Even in the remote Pomeroon regions of Guyana we see the same polarizing tendency. Magda, a black prostitute, and Cristo, her son--wanted by the police for alleged murder-- function as scapegoats for society. The village and its police stand for order, while the prowling tiger in the jungle expresses the threat to order. Similarly the self-image of moral purity, success, and cultural superiority held by the white population is at once made possible, and threatened, by the guilt of Magda and Cristo. The novel moves from a rigid polarization to a symbol marriage of opposites in the union of black Cristo with white Sharon. It concludes in anticipation of a new order ushered in by the birth of Sharon's child.

Significantly, in this novel Harris chooses a region of Guyana that was never in fact appropriated by Europeans, one bare of the physical architecture of the plantation. The West Indian, Harris says, "lives in a comparatively bare world ... where the monumental architecture of the old world is the exception rather than the rule. Yet the values of that very old world have still imposed themselves evidently on his cultural patterns and economic way of life."[29] In choosing this particular region for his setting, Harris points directly to a metaphysical rather than a physical plantation landscape. "We have never had here the Dutch, English, French hide-bound imperialist," Cristo tells Sharon, but continues, "We've had our imperialist, the same pattern of blue blood and true; mixed with yellow and black. Our own parents and our blind scraping grandparents" (p. 115). It is a human, not an exclusively racist propensity that Harris describes, and appropriately he has his society make a scapegoat of Sharon, the lily-white virgin, as well as of black Magda and Cristo.

The story of *The Whole Armour* is quickly told, chiefly because it is the interstices of action, not action itself, that are important in Harris's vision. Magda, seeking to save her son, Cristo, from being apprehended by the police for alleged murder of a rival suitor to Sharon--a well-educated, lily-white virgin living in the village--asks the recluse Abram, one of her clients, to conceal the boy in the hut he occupies away from the village down by the shore. In an angry altercation with the youth, Abram suddenly collapses and dies, and while Cristo is off to seek Magda's advice, his corpse is dragged into the jungle by a tiger. Magda, returning with Cristo, finds the mangled and rotting corpse, and insists that Cristo don Abram's clothes. Armed with her fiction that Cristo is dead and that Abram has gone to hunt the tiger in the jungle, Magda returns to the village and arranges a wake for her son. At the wake another angry exchange ends in another death--the stabbing of Mattias, Sharon's present suitor, by Peet, her father. Cristo, clothed in the skin of a tiger, returns to the wake, and is joined by Sharon in his final flight into the forest. There the two, exiled as scapegoats--he for murder and as one who is dead, she as a witch for whom three youths have lost their lives--experience a sense of inner wholeness, of "communitas" with each other and the society from which they sprang, and a oneness with nature itself, all symbolized in a sexual union that must be one of the most lyrical moments in West Indian writing. After the two discover the body of Peet, who has committed suicide, Magda arrives, urgently warning them to escape from the police who, undeceived, are now in search of Cristo. To his mother's horror, Cristo, who as had a visionary experience during his forty days in the forest, decides to hand himself over to justice, leaving Sharon to bring forth the child she has conceived through his embrace.

The community that Harris depicts has its own ritual boundaries expressing the ideology of the dominant group. The fictional self-image of each person is like armor, yet that armor is never "whole." Energies are directed into "the rallying of all their forces into an incestuous *persona* and image and alliance"--an identity that is "the very antithesis of their dark truth and history, written in the violent mixture of races that had bred them as though their true mother was a wanton on the face of the earth and their true father a vagrant and rogue from every continent" (p. 49).

The racial segregation of the villagers, reinforced by moral segregation (white virgin, black prostitute) becomes a metaphor for the rejection of the hidden self within each man--his past, his guilt, his desire. This dual self, mask and face, is projected onto the outer landscape of social structure even though beyond society's boundaries the natural world acknowledges no such polarizations--ebb and flow, waxing and waning, accretion and erosion being the ongoing dialectical rhythms of nature.

Death conducts us from this structured world of polarities into a betwixt and between, a limbo where the constructs of social ordering are lost and the face behind the mask now appears. The wake that Magda holds for Cristo occupies the central portion of the novel, and it is in this shared experience of whatever lies beyond life that individuals in the village confront their hidden selves. In so doing they see their true relatedness to each other and to a past of which they are ashamed. Abram's dream in fact prepares us for this vision and provides the tree image that will become one of the key symbols of the text. Abram's dream is of an inverted tree:

Abram dreamed he was crawling in a wood--on the high branches of a tree--and had reached the extremity of a curious twisted limb. The leaves of the tree turned into black swooping birds, obscene and terrifying. He surveyed what appeared to be a beach beneath him, on which lay an old rotted tree-trunk, or ancient tacouba, hard as iron. He knew he must jump, but felt he would cripple himself in landing upon it. He sprang from his perch, meeting softer ground than he had expected, astonished to see the entire tree above him, its roots spread-eagled in the air, naturally and invisibly cradled and supported. (p. 17)

The dream, with its imagery of decay, foreshadows Abram's death, yet points to his misconception of the nature of death itself, which proves to be the inverse of his expectations--a cradle of life. Anticipating the novel's movement, the dream implies that the tiger of death (both literal and metaphoric) is a fiction, and that the mortal wounds we dread actually lead us into life.

The tree, universally accepted as an image of a cyclical cosmic regeneration and as a symbol of the link between earth and heaven, takes on a particular significance in the sacred Vedic texts of Hinduism, where it is depicted as inverted, drawing its sustenance from the sun.[30] This Eastern picture of reciprocity and of inverted order invites a deconstruction of accepted categories. Initially, as for Abram in his reluctance to enter the void of uncertainty, the limbo of non-being, such an inversion is filled with terror, but later, for Sharon and Cristo, driven from social order and freed from their false images into a new creative selfhood, it is a miracle revealed. The tree image in the following section summarises its density of import in this novel as a challenge to the authority of any one-sided point of view:

The stern winter of hardship had yielded to the spring of fertility but the roots and branches of transformation descended and arose only in the starred eye of love. For all who were blind to this miraculous dawning frailty the new time appeared only when it manifested an iron shell and proportion, rigid as the grave season that was past, inexplicable as all time before, and unhuman as the rhythm of the tides on the earth, and the trunk of triumphant prosperity became--in this context--a recurring fate and epitaph rather than the ascension of everlasting thanks-giving. (p. 99)

Abram's dream is of death, but his death-fall makes possible Cristo's life. Harris here invokes what he has dubbed "myths of catastrophe"--universal myths showing catastrophe to be the gateway to a higher plane of blessedness.[31] The myth alluded to is that of the patriarch Abraham, whose story, recontexualized in Christian exegesis, foreshadows the sacrifice by Almighty God of his Son. Abram/Abraham experiences blessedness following catastrophe in the fulfillment of God's promise of descendants innumerable as the stars to be born from Sarah's "dead" womb.

(Stars figure prominently in this novel.) The catastrophe in God's demand that Abram sacrifice his son and that each firstborn be circumcised is imaged in the ubiquitous "wounds" of the narrative, while "wounds" and "tree" taken together announce the Crucifixion. Yet death is not the end: for the "flying seed" born of the "complex bizarre womb of Abram" promises future generations. In a characteristic of liminal paradox, male/female distinctions are lost, and a vision is born of the material world as a tomb/womb in which the eternal Spirit of life is perennially incarnate. Thus, although his body dies, Abram's spiritual presence curiously haunts the text, as the barrier between life and death melts away, and tomb/womb become one--transforming the stench of putrefaction into the fragrance of blossom.

The ritual of the wake itself is a rite of passage between the polarized realms of life and death, and it is here that rigid concepts crumble. Magda's home, a darkened upper room above a brightly lit yard, is, like the village within the forest, a signifying landscape that mirrors the shadowy repressed psyche of the villagers, contrasting as it does the lighted world of the persons or mask within the shadowy anima or hidden self: "A single lantern was hanging behind her, dim, accentuating a wave of shadows crowding the house, still abstracts, they appeared at times cast up through the floor by the living souls that stopped and seethed again in the brilliant bottomyard under her feet" (p. 50). In this passage, Harris, with great economy, transforms a common enough Guyanese setting, the open "bottom house" beneath raised living quarters, into a mythic network of inverted images representing the mirror--reflection of the self concealed behind the masking persona. Dominating this scene of reflection is "the compulsive oblique mirror of Magda's countenance": the face of the whore reflecting society's image.

Magda's mirroring face represents that dangerous threshold between truth and fiction. Sacred whore and social outcast, she personifies the liminal. Magda bears the unendurable pain of being "a vicarious scavenger and vulture of men, describing in the wilderness their witness and dream of purification" (p. 53). Again the "pivoting of sacredness" and the danger of liminality appears in the meeting of "upright" society with social outcast: "There was something superstitiously holy about such an unholy woman," the villagers feel, and as Magda watches them come to her wake, her "royal purple gown" expresses symbolically the "sovereignty she had exercised upon them in their weakness" (p. 50). In her person are summed up the ambivalent attitudes of man to woman; she is either goddess or witch, either "an unattainable idol that stood on the highest blossom in the world or . . . a compulsive fantastic whore with its black roots in the wilderness" (p. 87). But as Sharon, the pure "snow-maiden" of folk myth, sees herself in Magda, we become aware of the falsity of such dualities: "She stared into the dim room, hesitating for a moment when she saw Magda's countenance, for all the world like a dark flickering terrible mirror reflecting every dim consciousness in the house. Sharon wondered if the face she saw was her own bemused vision" (pp. 77-78).

Like Sharon, the guests at the wake, one by one, confront the darkness that in their daily lives they repress. Mattias, who considers himself "free of the past as of every beggarly origin," faces not only the grandfather who begged and peddled to amass what has become the family fortune, but deeper issues, too. Accused by Peet of having sexual relations with Sharon, he finds himself "challenged by the wake--to discern a deep irrational logic on the most troubling question of all mankind--the meaning of individual innocence and guilt" (p. 70). As he contemplates this mystery, he stands on the "threshold of profound participation" in the "walking tree and family of mankind," and sinks into a deathlike "limbo" experience where all his certainties are shaken.

But the void of uncertainty is not the end. Sharon, for instance, stripped of the comforting fiction of her image as sacred white virgin and cast outside of society's margins as a witch, moves, under Cristo's shamanistic tutelage, from misconception into a true "conception" resulting from the union of her "light" and Cristo's "shadow." Harris, following Jung, speaks of this moment of entering the void as being painfully disorienting; Sharon, we read, "felt she was suffocating and dying on a scaffold--crushed in the arms of a wild beast" (p. 84). This embrace of the "tiger," though, is in fact the embrace of a god, and she is "in the arms of the universal bridegroom of love, pierced by all the ecstasy of constructive innocence" (p. 85). One aspect of Sharon's crucifixion is Peet. Her initial impulse is to run headlong from this man who is at once her father and a symbol of the vile trade in human flesh that is the story of Guyana's past. The vomit-stained dollar bills littering Magda's home represent not only Peet's sexual lust, but the commerce in human beings and their suffering which constitute the "peat" out of which this lovely (Rose of) Sharon has sprung. Peet's bills symbolize, too, the impulse that affirms the self by negating the other; it is a good investment to maintain the transgressor in his "sin" so that one appears more righteous by contrast.

But this represents only one facet of Peet. As Sharon moves beyond the "moon-struck world" of black/white assumptions, she sees another side of her father, and catches a glimpse of the mythic character of his actions. Peet is capable of grieving for a beloved wife and venting his anger over her death on his unborn son and, consequently, against Sharon's suitors who, he feels, "would eat their own mother alive for a chance to survive" (p. 93). Suddenly Sharon sees Peet as he might have been, the shadow behind the man: "Sharon saw the spirit of her father for the first true organic time . . . *this* was what he might have been. It made her feel someone should have known how to climb into him with the beauty of all compassion" (p. 86). Slipping from the Gestalt form of Peet as the sum of his visible actions to an undifferentiated presencing of the whole man as he is in his spirit, we see a totally different person. By ignoring the fiction of his acts in time and focusing on his person manifesting itself in the silences between those acts we realize that the disreputable old drunk who limps across our vision is no other than Legba, god of the crossroads and marketplace, dying so that new life can be born.

The boundaries between what was and what might have been are completely blurred as Sharon is led by Cristo to look at Peet's body as it hangs in death, suspended (significantly) from the skylight. As she faces the stark horror of death, all her defenses break. She has seen already that a man's acts and appearances in "serial time" are a mere fiction. Now Cristo takes her a step further to understand that the physical itself is an illusion, a false image: "No use digging up anything like that, you hear me. Because it's only worth a damn when it shelters one's free spirit" (p. 111). The body itself is a "shell," a "pregnant fortress." Man, too, Cristo sees, is part of the cycle of nature, of an endless metamorphosis, and, regardless of his achievements and progress, mutability characterizes his existence; Sharon and Cristo understand that "their education had been paid for by the economics of regional instability, however far they may have appeared to have journeyed out of their father's land" (p. 111).

Harris's contextualizing of this passage about the unreality of the physical, and the fictive nature of death, makes it impossible for Cristo's instruction of Sharon to be read as an affirmation of Christian teaching on the hope of the resurrection. The self-reflexive quality of the novel clearly implies that each successive material construct is a fiction: each ordering of reality is a falsifying body of evidence that must yield to the greater reality it neglects. Only by standing outside of our fictions can we become free: "One would begin all over to perceive particulars of draughtmanship as never before--in the way one secretly observes (whether one knows it or not) a reflection in a mirror or a material portrait--by standing hypothetically outside of the dead time, with a capacity to make oneself perfectly aware and free" (p. 130). To climb out of our metaphors and view our past from the margins where alone irony is possible is to be "aware and free."

And so we turn, finally, to Cristo--criminal and fugitive, outcast from society. In his position of liminality Cristo fulfills the role of the mythic trickster or shaman. He is variously associated with Christ on the "gallows-tree," with Ogun in the dismemberment of his body, with the Amerindian shaman

ritually suffering in the wilderness to bring life and healing to
the tribe. Symbols of the ambiguity of his status proliferate. He
is both dead and alive, innocent and guilty; he is both man and
tiger, both himself and every runaway that has fled before
conquering forces. Murderer and life-giver, devil and savior,
violent rapist and bridegroom of love, he embodies every
dimension of the paradox that is human experience. In the
wilderness he is involved in an experience that is outside of time,
beyond the constructs of empirical certainties. He deals in
fiction, too, but unlike the fictions of Magda and the other
villagers, Cristo's fictions are an attempt to reveal, not conceal,
an underlying reality. Through the mock battle--a fiction staged
by the local Catholic mission--Cristo enters a reality of communion with the "shattered tribe," the "terrible broken family," to
which he belongs, and experiences in his own person the fragmentation and dismemberment of his race.

Yet dismemberment is not the end. He relates to Sharon how
the medicine men pieced together the broken fragments of his
person: "The medicine men . . . looked after me. Fitted me
together again. Chest and stump. Broken neck and skull" (p.
127-128). Out of the broken phallus of trickster, we understand,
plants and flowers spring to life; similarly, new life forms grow
from the broken body of Cristo. Clothed in the tiger skin he has
won by confronting the darkness, he now returns as healer of the
tribe, relating to Sharon the sacred myths of origins, leading her
through brokenness to a vision of wholeness. Cristo leaves the
black and white world of virgin and whore, civilized village and
untamed tiger, and Anancy-like he weaves new configurations,
denying the polarizations, destroying the old structure, and pieces
together a new world of living relationships. For as he tells his
tale to Sharon, morning breaks, and the spirit of Anancy, god of
creation, creates a new day, revealing a web that relates all things
to each other and to their center in perfection of balance and
harmony: "The spider of dawn had appeared and the moon had
far descended. The morning star spun its long frail threads to
touch scattered islands of cloud in a delicate wheel whose radii
and circumference   rolled on every high peak, foothill and
valley" (p. 98). Here is a vision of wholeness, of relatedness, of
fulfillment, which contrasts with the rigid dualities of the old
order that obtains in the plantation landscape of the villagers'
psyche. There, the "tiger" is relegated to the "jungle." Peet, for
instance, sees the monster in Magda (p. 57), in Cristo and Mattias
(p. 93); he hunts for it in monstrous places in jungle and swamp,
but fails to realize that the tiger is within: "Peet shrank from
exploring the navel of the world where the mate of all fantasy
was devouring the umbilical chord of a stolen life" (p. 91).
Magda, too, in her "sculptured" pose, cannot accept death, but
fights to the end to preserve her son, failing to realize that he has

attained a freedom that far transcends the ongoing mask-wearing, fugitive experience she seeks to grasp for him.

In contrast, Sharon and Cristo abandon the "armor" that defends a false self, and are broken but subsequently reshaped. Sharon, entering the void, felt that she "was being uprooted from all the fixed assumptions she had shared with everyone and everything into an order so tenuous and fleeting it aroused a terrible insubstantial uneasiness" (p. 102). Cristo, too, embraces the tiger as he confronts the darkness within himself, and his death is followed by triumph as the medicine men clothe him with the skin of the tiger--the "slain jaguar of death." Together, the two move into an experience of wholeness and freedom, outside of time, outside of society; they are one with all things, and the intricate web of being becomes a reality for them.

This vision, this gnosis, comes to Cristo through the medium of fiction, for the intertribal warfare that reveals his relatedness to the "shattered tribe" is a staged mock battle. Similarly, his own decapitation and headlong flight through the jungle are, perhaps, fictions--yet they, too, are a true revelation of his inner state. Vision and fiction are thus accorded higher standing than fact and empirical knowledge. Harris's world privileges dream and vision, the clearsightedness of irrationality and the richness of metaphor. Collapsing the frontier between fact and fiction, Harris, through Cristo, creates a new vision from the fragments.

The moment of oneness shared by Cristo and Sharon as they "step back" from the perceptual frame they have always privileged is, in Victor Turner's terminology, one of "communitas." Turner describes a structure/communitas dialectic in which society is seen alternately as "a differentiated, segmented system of structural positions" (where role and status are crucial) and as "a homogeneous, undifferentiated *whole*" (where individuals are free and equal). Major liminal situations are described by Turner as "occasions on which a society takes *cognizance of itself* or rather where, in an interval between their incumbence of specific fixed positions, members of that society may obtain an approximation, however limited, to a global view of man's place in the cosmos and his relations with other classes of visible and invisible entities."[32] Thus, in moving to the margins of what is socially accepted, Sharon and Cristo move into freedom. Despite the fact that Cristo is about to be arrested and executed, Sharon knows that he "would be free in the end . . . in an armour superior to the elements of self-division and coercion" (p. 134). Claude Levi-Strauss, in *Tristes Tropiques*, describes precisely this experience:

The man who wishes to wrest something from Destiny must venture into that perilous margin-country where the norms of Society count for nothing and the demands and guarantees of

the group are no longer valid. He must travel to where the
police have no sway .... Once in this unpredictable border-
land a man may . . . acquire for himself, from among the
immense repertory of unexploited forces which surrounds any
well-regulated society, some personal provision of power.[33]

But the characters are not the only ones who go through a rite
of passage; the reader also experiences his own wilderness
journey. Disoriented by the disrupted and overlapping chronology, by the absence of secure spatial boundaries between solid
objects, by the sense of being suspended between realism and
symbol, between the mimetic and the mythic, sign and signifier,
and a host of other liminal phenomena, the reader gropes for a
foothold--unable to take refuge in any known literary landmarks.

Disorientation occurs because formal continuities and reader
anticipations are repeatedly disrupted. The plot line, instead of
dominating, recedes into the background. Privileged ground is
yielded to what takes place "between the acts." The protagonist
is plural: a composite of the folk and of nature itself. One might
argue that the protagonist is, in fact, the spirit of creativity,
Anancy, breaking through every dead shell into triumphant new
life. Harris in one breath celebrates the ongoing splendor of
natural creation and the same creative energy in man himself.
Each reader has the capacity to be a creative "womb" out of
which the "Other" is reborn.

Characterization, too, takes on a new dimension when we find
not only that characters change dramatically as we see more of
them, or see them from a different vantage point, but that they
merge into one another and even into the landscape itself, as in
this passage where Sharon embraces Cristo:

The feeling in her stroking fingers made her see far away
across the moonlit river--as if she rode in the beam of light-sli-
ding hollows and rising features, growing into stones and
foot-hills. It was along this very mysterious backbone and
watershed--between frightful jaguar and newborn love--that
the frightful jaguar of death had roamed, leaping across
emotional tumbling rivers from crag to crag, across Devil's
Hole Rapids and the Nameless Falls, greenheart ravines
steaming with mist, blue mountains frowning in cloud, coming
from as far as the heart of Brazil into Venezuela's Orinoco and
Guiana's Potaro, Mazaruni, Cuyuni and Pomeroon. Her fingers
travelled across the map of Cristo's skin, stroking the veins in
every ancestor's body.(p. 88)

Such a passage suggests that Harris gives greater weight to
relationships than to separate entities. The western, post-Cartesi-
an way of approaching the world has been a process of isolating,

classifying, breaking down into components. But the opposite can be said of Harris's method. The continual overlapping of edges in his work--his intertextuality, the merging of character with character and of character with landscape, and the backdrop of nature's mutability (eroded boundaries, seasonal change, birth and death)--such overlapping expresses an ideological stance that points to the limitations of Western ontology.

Heidegger, in his *Poetry, Language, and Thought*, discusses scientific ontology before replacing it with his own phenomenological approach. The scientifically oriented method is always an assault on the object, he says, even in aesthetics. Conceiving of the "thing" as a "bearer of traits, as the unity of a manifold of sensations, as formed matter," Western methods fail to reach the "thingliness of the thing." Our very mode of perception is faulty, he asserts: "This long-familiar mode of thought preconceives all immediate experience of beings. The preconception shackles reflection on the being of any given entity." True, he admits, the current concept of the thing will always fit; nevertheless, "it does not lay hold of the thing as it is in its own being, but makes an assault upon it."[34] To correct such misapprehensions of the "thing," we need, according to Heidegger, to let the thing "display its thingly character directly . . . yield ourselves to the undisguised presence of the thing."[35] For everything resists assault: "Earth shatters every attempt to penetrate into it. It causes merely calculating importunity upon it to turn into a destruction."[36] What is crucial is the "step back":

> When and in what way do things appear as things? They do not appear *by means* of human making. But neither do they appear without the vigilance of mortals. The first step toward such vigilance is the step back from the thinking that merely represents--that is, explains-- to the thinking that responds and recalls.
>
> The step back from the one thinking to the other is no mere shift of attitude. It can never be any such thing for this reason alone: that all attitudes, including the ways in which they shift, remain committed to the precincts of representational thinking . . . . The step back takes up its residence in a co-responding which, appealed to in the world's being, answers within itself to that appeal.[37]

Heidegger's term "co-responding" returns this discussion to Harris for his novels are a texture/weaving of co-respondences yielding to a reading that responds and recalls, but resisting the assault of formal analysis and explanation. Harris's own co-respondence with existing literary texts (as well as with other fields of human enterprise, notably his knowledge of land surveying) is astonishing. In this novel, as in all of his work, there is so much intertextuality that the very margins of the text disappear. Blake's and Yeats's tiger join the jaguar of South American folklore, and the Rose of Sharon and the "black but comely" spouse from the *Song of Solomon* reappear in a new context. Magda is a reborn Mary Magdalene anointing Christ's feet with an ointment whose fragrance fills the house, and the Oedipus myth is invoked in the repeated allusions to incest and patricide. These constitute merely a sampling of the literary allusions, and the folklore allusiveness is just as rich: the tale of the snow maiden, the figure of the witch, Earth mother, Legba and Anancy (or is the web Penelope's?), and the multiform rites of passage.

The very fabric of the text makes numerous statements. The absence of an epic hero is an implicit rejection of a particular approach to historical record. The emphasis on dream, vision, memory, and myth, together with the metaphysical bent, pull away from the thing-oriented, materialistic world of empiricism to a worldview which recognizes a deeply hidden order mocking the limitations of our rigid forms and concepts. Even the defiance in Harris's choice of setting--an obscure region in an obscure Third World country--is an assertion of the value of "naked, unaccommodated man," pitted against the "monumental architecture," of his achievements and a social structure bearing down to annihilate him.[38] In this novel, then, Harris establishes his "plantation landscape" within the prejudiced worldview of his protagonists, both black and white, who seek to preserve a given, though false, structure. His fiction plunges the reader into a limbo where characters in the action (if not the reader himself) come to see the limitations of their cherished concepts. The liminal zone, as I have repeatedly emphasized, is the sacred topos where ritual initiation takes place and myths of origin are revealed. Social structuring is negated by a pervasive trickster spirit hovering where order ends and chaos begins. The novel does not end in destruction, though. Out of the dream-chaos is created a new, visionary world order. Implicitly we are required to ask whether utopia is reached through structure or through movement into communitas, whether the material or the metaphysical will be the means of attaining our hopes, whether to stride into the future or return to the past. Perhaps, too, we are to consider whether or not all our utopia dreams are not just that--dreams, fictions that must be destroyed before we can be truly free. Perhaps the kingdom of God is indeed already among us if we have eyes to see. We turn finally to a theme that is to occupy Harris increasingly in later novels: the work of art itself. The repeated references to mirrors, reflections, fictions, writing, and painting underline his metafictive position--the artist standing on the margins of his own art in reflective irony. Harris has himself mentioned his interest in the theories of

Anton Ehrenzweig.[39] Ehrenzweig's discussion of the dialectic process of artistic creation--the swing between Gestalt forms and an "oceanic level of dedifferentiation" is significant as we relate it to the method of Harris's own text.

Ehrenzweig argues that the particular gift of the creative mind is its ability to stand back from the canvas of Gestalt forms, allowing the fancy to sink to an "oceanic level of dedifferentiation" where ambivalence prevails and no one form is privileged at the expense of another. From this formlessness, new and alternative forms can be created. Repeatedly in Harris's fiction one remarks the dialectical swing between structure and antistructure, between event and reflection. It is the impossibility of capturing the spirit of life in art forms (or in any of our perceptual frames) that preoccupies him in the person of Cristo, who lies in Sharon's lap "still dreaming of the painted surfaces of life, the spirit of nature that always escapes from the canvas even as it invokes the budding schools of idolatry and thought" (p. 130).

Given such a clear metafictive hint, the reader must place the theme of patricide in a new context. Going back to Freud's totem-taboo, one sees the slaying of the literary "father"--an act through which the "son" paradoxically deifies him--as a continuous process of literary creation. The artist at once slays and immortalizes his predecessor in the act of misprision (to use Bloom's term).[40] "Cristo's legacy to his son was the legacy of every ancestral ghost--the appraisal as well as the execution of the last fiction in time" (p. 130). And so we come full circle. The "spirit of place" that haunts Harris's work cannot be trapped in art, in man's structures of permanence. Life, like the natural landscape of Guyana, is in constant metamorphosis--waxing and waning, ebbing and flowing, dying to be reborn. Yet man must build his "Houses." Hena Maes-Jelinek, commenting on Mohammed's "palace" in *The Far Journey of Oudin*, says that "for Wilson Harris the finished house (the 'palace' Mohammed wants for himself) is only a symbol of material welfare and dangerous consolidation of power whereas the never-ended construction invokes a pattern of life unceasingly making and unmaking itself."[41] Like Mohammed, man longs for a palace. In his art, his culture, his religion, his social mask-wearing, he repeatedly attempts to make permanent that which is forever in flux, striving endlessly and tragically for utopia, city of God/gold, a "whole" armor to protect his human frailty.

The Great House, its surrounding land, and the dangerous margins where master and slave meet--itself a landscape inscribed wherever Europe set foot in the "Third" or New World--is worked by Lamming and Harris into a paradigm not only of First and Third World relations but also of an impulse in the heart of every man. This impulse is arbitrarily to privilege and denigrate in

order to preserve a biased conceptual order. Mythically conceived, the Great House and its surrounds becomes a polysemous
signifier. The model I have described works toward social
criticism and yet reaches into realms of the psychological,
existential, and aesthetic. Within its geographies of significance,
the artist, identifying always with the folk, works to invert,
deconstruct, and unname. The response of both Harris and
Lamming to tradition's polarizations is inspired by an enduring
folk consciousness--a consciousness preserved through rites of
passage that lead into antistructure. Lamming's major metaphor
for this process is the Haitian Ceremony of Souls, while Harris's
major renaming takes its force from overlapping myths of
catastrophe drawn from many cultures. Both authors use the
local landscape as well as a variety of mental states in order to
create, through imagery, a liminal zone of broken boundaries,
where creation can begin again.

NOTES

1. "History is built around achievement and creation; and
nothing was created in the West Indies," V. S. Naipaul, *The
Middle Passage* (London: Andre Deutsch, 1962), p. 29.
2. Mircea Eliade, *Myth and Reality* (New York: Harper and
Row, 1963), p. 12.
3. Morse Peckham, *Man's Rage for Chaos* (New York:
Schocken Books, 1967), p. 313.
4. Ibid., p. 314.
5. Wilson Harris discusses the political implications of
writing such revolutionary fiction in the following excerpt from
his essay "History, Fable, and Myth in the Caribbean and the
Guianas," in *Anagogic Qualities of Literature*, ed. Joseph P. Strelka
(University Park and London: Pennsylvania State University
Press, 1971), pp. 121-131:

Therefore the rise of the poet or artist incurs a gamble of the
soul which is symbolized in the West Indian trickster (the
spider or anancy that creates an individual and personal risk
absolutely foreign to the conventional sanction of an old tribal
world: a risk which identifies the artist with the submerged
authority of dispossessed alchemic resources to conceal as well
as elaborate, a far-reaching order of the imagination which,
being suspect, could draw down upon him a crushing burden of
censorship in economic or political terms). He stands therefore
at the heart of both the lie of community and the truth of
community. And it is, I believe, in this trickster gateway--this
gamble of the soul--that there emerges the hope for a profoundly compassionate society committed to freedom within a

creative scale.

6. Mary Douglas, *Purity and Danger* (London: Routledge and Kegan Paul, 1966), p. 96. Moving from the premise that "dirt is essentially disorder; there is no such thing as absolute dirt," Douglas argues that "our pollution behavior is the reaction which condemns any object or idea likely to confuse or contradict cherished classifications." The ambiguities that are excluded as pollutants are, however, possessed of dangerous power, which, if channelled correctly (i.e., in framed ritual situation), can become a source of creative renewal.

7. Wilson Harris, *Tradition, the Writer and Society* (London: New Beacon Publications, 1967), p. 48.

8. Douglas, *Purity and Danger*, p. 104.

9. Arnold Van Gennep, *The Rites of Passage*, trans. Monika B. Vizedom (Chicago: University of Chicago Press, 1960), p. 18.

10. Wilson Harris, *The Whole Armour* (London: Faber and Faber, 1962; reprint, London: Faber and Faber, 1973), author's note, p. 8.

11. According to Philip Sherlock, during the sixteenth century, Spanish settlers in the West Indies brought livestock that destroyed Arawak cultivation. Some of the livestock became wild--*cimarrones*, that is, wild herds inhabiting the *cima* (summits). In Jamaica, groups of runaway slaves banded together in the mountain areas and were known as maroons.

12. Douglas, *Purity and Danger*, pp. 94-95.

13. The *tonelle* is the sacred space cleared for the Ceremony of Souls of Haitian vodun, a ritual in which souls of the dead are released into a higher plane of existence. The Ceremony's symbolic significance pervades Lamming's work, and is, indeed, central to *Season of Adventure*.

14. Victor Turner discusses in detail black, white, and red color symbolism in the rituals of the Ndembu people in *The Forest of Symbols* (Ithaca, N. Y.: Cornell University Press, 1967).

15. Douglas, *Purity and Danger*, p. 124.

16. Turner, *Forest*, p. 105.

17. Ibid., p. 99.

18. Hayden White, *Tropics of Discourse* (Baltimore: Johns Hopkins University Press, 1978), p. 128.

19. Ibid., p. 22.

20. Ibid., p. 19.

21. Ibid., p. 234.

22. Ibid., p. 233.

23. Walter Ong, *The Presence of the Word* (New Haven: Yale University Press, 1967).

24. I refer specifically to Walcott's "A Far Cry from Africa," *In a Green Night: Poems 1948-1960* (London: Jonathan Cape Ltd., 1969), p. 18.

25. Eliade, *Myth and Reality*, p. 160.

26. See Lamming's reading of *The Tempest* and his discussion of Prospero's gift to Caliban of language in *The Pleasures of Exile* (London: Michael Joseph, 1960).

27. Roland Barthes, *Mythologies*, trans. Annette Lavers (New York: Hill and Wang, 1972), p. 114.

28. Douglas, *Purity and Danger*, p. 4.

29. Harris, *Tradition*, p. 13.

30. See entry under *arbre*, *Dictionnaire des Symboles* (Paris: Seghers, 1969).

31. In an unpublished lecture entitled "The Uses of Myth," delivered at the University of Guyana in March 1978, Harris drew on the mathematical concept of happy-unhappy catastrophe to introduce his discussion of myths of catastrophe. In catastrophe myths, such as that of the many-armed Egyptian god Osiris, whose portrayal indicates a tragic dismemberment and a reassembling, Harris traced a moment existing in the most terrifying problem, which could lead to creative change. Creative response to such (partial) mythic motifs is set over against acceptance of and absorption into (total) authoritarian models. Harris, in effect, argued for an art that exposes the reader to the "originality of myth" in contradistinction to the "mimicry of fact."

32. Victor Turner, *Dramas, Fields, and Metaphors* (Ithaca, N. Y.: Cornell University Press, 1974), pp. 239-240.

33. Claude Levi-Strauss, *Tristes Tropiques* (New York: Atheneum, 1964), p. 41.

34. Martin Heidegger, *Poetry, Language, and Thought*, trans. Albert Hofstadter (New York: Harper, 1971), pp. 27-31.

35. Ibid., p. 25.

36. Ibid., p. 47.

37. Ibid., p. 182.

38. Harris, *Tradition*, p. 13.

39. Anton Ehrenzweig, *The Hidden Order of Art* (Berkeley: University of California Press, 1969).

40. Harold Bloom, *The Anxiety of Influence* (New York: Oxford University Press, 1973).

41. Hena Maes-Jelinek, *Wilson Harris* (Boston: G. K. Hall, 1982), pp. 24-25.

II

Clowns and Carnival

The House with its surrounding plantation can now be identified as a metonym not merely for the polarizations of colonialism, but for a variety of oppressive authoritarian structures. It names that propensity to impose an ideological worldview that denigrates and alienates others in an effort to promote itself. In the West Indies, history, language, and religion are structures encompassed by the House--subtle structures that privilege foreign, imported values and reject all that is natural and indigenous. The House and its plantation thus speaks of a dominant power using ideological structures to maintain its control. In Marxist terms, the House is the superstructure of European cultural forms, which the emergent energies of an economically exploited class experience as a monolithic architecture of oppression.

Between the House and its colonized landscape, though, lies a no-man's-land--a threshold between the two worlds. Intercourse between House/landlord and plantation/tenantry is highly charged; it bristles with danger. For it is in this limbo-void of dialectic that vital change can occur. Given the metaphorical inscriptions of the House in my model, one can, perhaps, understand why such architectural thresholds as walls and fences, kitchens and bathrooms (in that these guard what enters and leaves the body) should be marked by ideological conflict. One can see, too, why images of sexuality, fertility, growth, and energy are set against images of fixity, permanence, stasis, and sterility. For in the falsifying binary structure premised between House and folk, inevitable conflicts arise as the assumptions of Western materialism are challenged by the perhaps inarticulate aspirations, values, and creative impulses of a repressed and exploited folk. The conflict is not resolved simply by evicting the original tenant of the House and giving the lease to those formerly outside. The House has to be broken down; the entire polarizing structure of inside/outside, above/below, sacred/profane has to be demolished. Certainly the work of Lamming and Harris includes an attack on the economic and cultural privilege that the House assumes, but it goes far beyond to a "deconstruction" of the very epistemological foundations on which Western ideological structures rest.

Insofar as the fictive text challenges epistemological and ontological assumptions, its discourse abuts on that of the "real" world of political ideology. For ideologies and texts alike are "readings" of reality. In the absence of a fixed paradigm, seriality--readings upon readings--is all that remains to us. Such postmodernist concerns are faced implicitly and tentatively by Lamming, squarely and explicitly by Harris, as these two writers investigate what it means to read and reread the text, laying bare, as they do so, the conceptualizing process that seems only to trap us in a world of binary oppositions.

Aware of the structures imposed on both the topographical and psychic landscapes of the Third World, George Lamming and Wilson Harris seek to describe a process whereby a new world can be created from the ruins of an ideologically divided old one. Their novels are, in fact, self-conscious representations of the process of creation itself. In them, the artist-creator, whether as character in the fiction or its narrator, is the subject of the novel's discourse, And in the fictions of these two writers, the artist-creator always inhabits the antistructural boundaries of the houses of culture. In the present chapter, we shall examine the fictive contours of this liminal creator. The artist in the plantation model is a mediator of self-knowledge--a self-knowledge that comes only when one steps outside familiar conceptual structures in ironic contemplation.

Continuing the anthropological emphasis of my preceding chapter, the present discussion invokes more explicitly the folk figure of the mythic trickster, inhabitant of crossroads, marketplaces, and thresholds. Commencing with a survey of the trickster's characteristics and functions, my discussion moves to an analysis of the spirit and technique of the trickster in the artist-creators inhabiting the fictive landscapes of Lamming's *Season of Adventure* and *In the Castle of My Skin*, and Harris's *Genesis of the Clowns*. The goal of the present discussion is to analyze the techniques employed by two "folk" novelists as they deal with their own peculiar experience of the Great House.

Trickster, that baffling figure of folklore, is universal. Details of his origins and activities vary, but an inexplicable similarity exists in the various expressions of this criminal culture-hero. Trickster is the very embodiment of paradox. He is a violator of taboo, a perpetrator of incestuous relationships, and an illicit handler of excrement, menstrual blood, snot, urine, and other tokens of the body's margins. The taboo items that he handles reflect the trickster's situation as marginal to the social "body." He defies authority, parodies and criticizes social structure, and indulges in acts of aggression, destruction, and vindictiveness. Yet the asocial, independent trickster is also tied to society as a source of health and creativity. He is often the hero who brings "medicine" (i.e., supernatural power) to the tribe. Further, his typically gross phallicism is an expression of creative potential. Comic and life-affirming, he is a key ceremonial figure as he trades in deceit and ritually inverts social order. Isolated because of his taboo violations, he is nonetheless bound to society as its disciplinarian and sacrificial figure.[1]

Trickster's ambiguous status is a function of "structuring." For structuring always implies marginality--exclusion as well as inclusion. The solemnity and univocal certainties embodied in kingship, for example, invite the mocking, multivocal questioning of the Fool. And, as Barbara Babcock argues (adopting a phrase of Aldous Huxley's), social structuring requires a "tolerated margin of mess" where a creative mind, released from restraints of conformity, may reshape the world.[2] Universally, trickster creates chaos by his violation of sacred boundaries, but he also initiates a transformative process that turns "dung" into "medicine," a broken phallus into plants and flowers, and contradictory elements into a web of meaningful relationships.

Trickster is a master of commerce and exchange. Taking his position at meeting points--marketplace, thresholds, crossroads-- he faces both ways in perpetual ambiguity, inviting, even provoking intercourse between inside and outside. His insistence on social intercourse, on commerce across the boundaries of structured concepts, is symbolized variously in his aggressive sexuality, his mastery of language, and his trickiness in trade. Of the Fon trickster, Robert Pelton says: "Legba knows the words creative of intercourse, sexual and heavenly, ritual and economic, and everywhere his phallus stands as symbol of muteness overcome and communion re-established."[3]

Not surprisingly, given his capacity to hide in rafters and weave his web in any nook or cranny, Ananse, the spider of Ashanti folklore, survived the middle passage, and still spins his yarns throughout the Caribbean (as well as in the southern states of America). His survival in folk imagination surely has to do with his capacity to transform disruption, discontinuity, broken-ness, and defeat into triumphant new configurations of pos-sibility. His perennial rebellion and his use of comic trickery and deceit to expose the inadequacies of authority figures must surely have endeared him to the imagination of a downtrodden people. Oppressive structure creates a tragic vision in which a scapegoat or expiatory victim is necessary. Trickster, by contrast, belongs to the world of comic vision, of communitas and laughter: he "elude[s] the sacrifice or banishment that would affirm order at . . . (his) expense."[4] It is the triumph of the trickster-artist to so deconstruct and invert the given "text" of authority that the scapegoat of tragedy turns the tables on authority and emerges in a comedy of ironic reversal.

Pelton relates the tale of Ananse and a certain Mr. Hate-to-be--Contradicted in which Ananse triumphs ultimately by tricking the figure of presumptuous authority into actually contradicting himself. Ananse "negates negation and thereby gives birth to a dialectic whose aim is not synthesis, but a never-ending juggling of thesis and antithesis."[5] The name Hate-to-be-Contradicted, takes us back to the architectural solidity of the Great House. It is from the wild, untamed realm of paradox, uncertainty, ambiguity, and imagination beyond the fixed certainties of Western norms that the Caribbean artist, Ananse-fashion, brings the brokenness of folk experience together into a web of meaning and exposes the folly and danger of assuming a position of final authority.

Trader par excellence, Ananse "enters the human world to make things happen, to recreate boundaries, to break and re-establish relationships, to reawaken consciousness of the presence and the creative power of both the sacred Center and the formless Outside. Then he returns to that hidden threshold which he embodies and makes available as a passage to 'save the people from ruin.'"[6] Ananse, or Anancy as he becomes in the Caribbean, is a particularly compelling image of the artist. The spider and his web recur visibly throughout Harris's work as a kind of signature left playfully by the artist. Though invisible in Lamming's novels, Anancy is nevertheless omnipresent in spirit-- and very busy.

Given the cosmopolitan character of the Caribbean population, it is important to notice, too, that the spider is a universally recognized symbol, related particularly to the act of creation.[7] In India, the spider, weaving a web from her own substance, is associated with the sun, secreting its own rays, giving life from its own being, and relating all things, like an umbilical cord, to the center or principle of life. The sacred *Upanishads* speak of the spider gaining liberty by climbing up the thread it has spun from its own being. (Certainly an alluring image for the existential implications of "authoring" oneself through the narrative thread of the text.) In Africa and among the Incas of Peru (here we recall Harris's interest in South American folklore) the spider is used in divination, and the web that he spins is recognized as a system of signs--hence Anancy's skill with words. The Ashanti hold that Ananse, in defiance of Nyame, the sky god, created the sun, moon and stars, and man himself. He is also man's intercessor with Nyame. Classical Greece, too, gave a mythological place to the spider. Ariadne (from whose name the French language has the word *araignee*--spider) challenged Athena to a weaving contest. Athena, in her tapestry, portrays the gods in majesty. Ariadne, though, reveals her trickster bent toward contradiction when, in caricature and parody, she depicts the gods lovemaking with mortals. To escape Athena's fury, Ariadne hangs herself, but is turned into a spider by Athena (and once again the notion of salvation gained by way of the woven thread appears). Clearly the leap from Athena, goddess of wisdom, to Mr. Hate-to-be-Contradicted is not great--nor are we far from the authority, assumed wisdom, and power of the political and cultural imperialism suggested by the Great House.

Spider-man Anancy is, I am suggesting, a folk embodiment of that carnivalesque spirit that challenges imposed authority structures. And he is much more. In his mask wearing, his verbal ingenuity, his interstitiality, his savior role, and his multiethnic origins, spider Anancy is a profoundly significant naming of a strategy employed by the deprived to deal with the exploiter. Not surprisingly the Caribbean artist, as I shall show, is informed and guided by this trickster spirit as by a Muse, and the techniques of both Lamming and Harris have clearly sprung from a mental landscape in which interstitiality is a fertile space for a renaming of the world.

In this chapter, then, we will allow our eyes to wander to the hidden crevices and corners of the House to contemplate the spider, spinning its web secretly and silently, as a constant reminder of a life beyond the limits of solid and apparently permanent structures. Affirming life, rebelling against the negation of itself, recognizing the mutability of experience, yet drawing the world together in a moment of pattern, the spider with its web contrasts sharply with the fixity of the architectural monument. He reminds us, too, that when the House has fallen, the busy weaving of spiders will go on--testimony to an enduring and always marginal creativity. Man's task of creation is forever only beginning.

Trickster wears a mask because his activities violate sacred codes of conduct in society. He both criticizes and inverts the status quo. As Laura Makarius puts it, tricksters "are the projection in myth of the magician who violates a taboo in order to satisfy the need and aspirations of his group. This act of transgression would be that which enabled the group, at some time in its history, to acquire the magical 'medicine' which plays a fundamental role in its magical and ritual life."[8] Similarly, clowns, earthly counterparts of the mythic trickster, have the violation of taboo as their very raison d'etre. They are consequently marginalized by society, but recognized as bringing a kind of salvation: "It is necessary that the breaker of taboo should be viewed as acting alone, even if for the benefit of all.

It is necessary that he should be conceived as 'the other,' in opposition to the group, even though he acts on their behalf. That is why when participating in ritual, the clown appears as an individualist--independent, social, non-integrated."[9] Clowns are made into expiatory figures who bear the guilt of normal men.

A fine instance of the artist figure presented as an expiatory victim of the order described by Makarius is found in *Season of Adventure* in the incident of the sale of "Jordan water." Chiki and others of the Boys are drafted to replace rural workers in America who, in turn, have been enlisted to fight in the war in Europe. Back in San Cristobal, land on which the folk have lived for generations has been appropriated by the Crown. In an effort to raise funds to repossess the land on behalf of his people, Chiki engages in a clownlike ritual plunder of the Virginian believers. Their eager response to his offer to baptize them in genuine, imported Jordan water is the measure of their unquestioning acceptance of a worldview that declares them unclean. Trickster-like, Chiki (cheeky?) introduces ambiguity into a realm of sacred assumption, and, through his violation of taboo, brings "medicine" to his people. But the restored "heritage" is far more than the land that his American dollars can purchase; it is the release from domination by imported, received values and an assertion of the inherent worth of the indigenous folk. In order to bring "medicine" to his tribe, Chiki suffers as a scapegoat; he still bears scars from a beating he received at the hand of the infuriated Virginians: "America brutalized his body, disfigured his face beyond the recognition of his nearest friends" and his blood "was pouring like the river of Jordan itself" (p. 189). Hounded by those whom he has baptized--those to whom he would bring new life and freedom--Chiki becomes a Christlike figure himself.

Formal religion, Lamming implies, tends to become another dead, houselike structure--serving the political interests of the elect few inside, and failing to minister to those it systematically excludes. Chiki and Gort, artists who expose themselves to danger in the cause of social justice, do not bear the name of saint (as do Agnes and Veronica), but are associated with Christ in the language of the text. Chiki's blood is the price of redemption of the land, and Gort's journey to stir up support for the protest march on Freedom Square is, in the narrator's eyes, "less painful, but no less arduous than the historic journey which that other man had chosen for his death on a public cross" (p. 350).

It is of interest to note in passing that theologian Harvey Cox argues in his study *The Feast of Fools* that Christ, himself, is the supreme trickster, who perennially is found outside the structures of religiosity:

Like the jester, Christ defied custom and scorns crowned heads.
Like a wandering troubadour he has no place to lay his head.

Like the clown in a circus parade, he satirizes existing
authority by riding into town replete with regal pageantry
when he has no earthly power. Like a minstrel he frequents
dinners and parties. At the end he is costumed by his enemies
in a mocking caricature of royal paraphernalia. He is crucified
amidst sniggers and taunts with a sign over his head that
lampoons his laughable claim.[10]

Cox's argument draws a parallel between the religious and the
aesthetic. Man wants a secure, closed system, but "God comes to
man as the disturber of his peace, the one who will not allow him
to settle down. The religious experience, like the aesthetic, is on
one level an experience of disorder, but it points to another
order, a city to come which, though it is never fully attained,
prevents man from being completely content with the present."[11]
Once truth and reality are recognized as being beyond man's
structures, greater than the historical dimension, the continual
"other than" to our ideological frames, then what remains is a
continuous play between the worlds of fact and the milieu of
fantasy--a chain of signifiers without a transcendent signified.
Homo ludens, homo festivus, homo fantasius now finds place in
a world that Puritanism and capitalism together have structured
on the premise of man as worker and producer. Christ, says Cox,
"is the spirit of play in a world of calculated utilitarian serious-
ness," and prayer is a kind of play--a fantasy activity releasing us
from the constraint of fact and requiring that we imagine other
situations than those existing in fact.[12] Art, too, one might
continue, is play--a celebration of the otherness that lies outside
each successive structure, a deconstructing of society's fictions.
Given this celebration of play as opposed to the political stress
on work, an otherwise meaningless episode in *Season of Adventure* becomes charged with significance. Just before Piggott and
his men come to arrest the Boys as suspects in Raymond's murder,
there is a lyrical moment when the entire yard is at play with an
inflated pig's bladder. It is a game of skill, a game involving
everyone, and the sole rule is to use only the head to keep the
"ball" in play: "In a matter of minutes the entire yard seemed
occupied with keeping the bladder aloft" (p. 255). The bladder
finally falls into a pot of crabs, whose "silent regiment of claws"
anticipates the police brutality that follows close on the festivity.
Angrily the womenfolk reproach their men for being out of
work, and again the moment of wholeness breaks into a divided
landscape in which work and play are mutually exclusive, and
work given the place of privilege.
In the context of San Cristobal's Puritan-capitalist ideology,
humanity is so reified that sexuality, the ultimate example of
play for its own sake, is exploited as a capital holding. Lamming
exposes the nineteenth-century political use of Christianity to

serve economic ends by allowing a missionary hymn of the period to be sung by a prostitute in a bar. The words "Work for the night is coming/When man's work is done" (p. 187) lose their intended meaning in the woman's mouth!

Since the word brought by missionaries has been drafted to sacralize political ideology, any attempt to displace that ideology involves a demystification of the word. Strategies to expose linguistic ambiguities are consequently abundant in the work of both Harris and Lamming. Harris's method is an unnaming --a movement to namelessness, which must precede a renaming of the self by the self. In Lamming's world we see that the use of code names (of individuals and bands) is a political strategy for survival in a situation where naming from outside has been the norm (one thinks of the string of names from a Christian text given to territories in the region). Caliban must move beyond cursing Prospero in the language Prospero has contained him in; he must lay bare the opacities of the word itself. And this he does by stepping outside of structure--by trading on the ambiguities of linguistic discourse.

One feature of clowns that Laura Makarius draws attention to deserves particular mention. She refers to the "backward speech" of clowns, their custom of talking in opposites; such speech, she says, "is the concomitant of a breach of taboo, because the latter likewise represents the reverse of normal, accepted behavior. Backward speech is meant to render this inversion manifest, and to underline it symbolically."[13] The linguistic trickery described by Makarius is also explored by the American critic Henry Louis Gates, Jr., who takes as his archetypal model for the black artist the Afro-American folk trickster, the signifying monkey. Gates discusses in detail the wordplay of the Afro-American in his daily speech, his oral tradition, and his art, and posits chiasmus as its chief characteristic: "The ironic reversal of a received racist image of the black as simianlike, the Signifying Monkey--he who dwells on the margins of discourse, ever punning, ever troping, ever embodying the ambiguities of language--is our trope for repetition and revision, indeed is our trope of chiasmus itself, repeating and simultaneously reversing in one deft, discursive act."[14] "Signifying," as Gates describes it, "is a rhetorical practice unengaged in information giving. Signifying turns on the play and chain of signifiers, and not on some supposedly transcendent signified."[15] Gates asserts that it is in charting such signifying practice--simultaneous repetition and revision of received "texts"--that a literary tradition is revealed.

Lacking an indigenous heritage of literary texts, the West Indian writer conducts this repetition and revision of received texts in a unique way. The available written texts are all alien to him--whether literary or historical, biblical or legal. But an alternative text is there--the unwritten text of memory and folktale, of landscape and plantation, of the vernacular and the calypso, of an inheritance of wisdom passed on through proverb and religious ritual. It is to this oral tradition that the writer turns: to the signifying spider-man outside the Great House of literary canonicity.

Chiki's revisionist, deconstructive activity is perhaps best seen in his inversions of the biblical text through his painting. Here he stands on the margins of a great tradition, but works old forms into new combinations in a kind of "*bricolage*."[16]   A chiasmus of repetition and revision appears in his depiction of biblical themes. His representation of Lazarus climbing back to life has a revised signification, juxtaposed as it is in the larger text of the novel with the theme of release brought to the souls of the dead in the Ceremony. Chiki's ritual reorganization of experience--like the ritual reshaping of landscape by the *houngan*--becomes the means by which the folk are released from the tomblike structure of Western signifying and given a voice.

Similarly, his depiction of the marriage of Cana, at which Christ turned water into wine, becomes (since marriage is something that concerns the Great--not the folk) an expression of carnival. Here deprivation is converted into plentiful abundance, and division into relatedness.

Chiki's final picture transforms Christ's parable of the man who buried his God-given talents into "Chiki's parable"--a dramatic inversion in which not the talents, but the man himself is buried beneath the ground, his crippled hand emerging from a "body of miraculous strength" to pull black leaves down with him. The head cannot see where "behind its burial the paint shines bright. An incredible harvest of yellow paint sprouts like a field of corn" (p. 230). Chiki's painting lays bare the paradox that Western adherents to Christianity, which celebrates the value of each man's talent, were in fact accomplices in a system that denied the "miraculous strength" of black creativity. For such adherents buried not merely talents, but men--millions of them--like so many black leaves in the ground. And the buried blindly acquiesce--yielding their bodies to produce a rich "golden" harvest for other reapers. Thus the Christian text is "read" no longer as a means of reinforcing social order (each man using his talents) but as a vehicle of social criticism, an assertion of a vital black heritage that still lies buried, denied expressivity by an arbitrarily imposed system.

Chiki's art, by introducing ambiguity, implicitly denies the existence of any transcendent or sacred signified, and insists instead on a multiplicity of signifiers that serve to correct and modify one another as assorted gods do in the *houngan*'s tent. Chiki's aim, like that of the trickster, is to introduce contradiction so that his themes "extracted from a Christian text, are now transformed into an opposite vision" (p. 188). He denies the word of authority, insisting on intercourse and dialogue.

Indeed, Lamming's preoccupation with the role of the artist in society places him at a crossroads in many ways. He implicitly explores, for instance, in his overlapping of various forms of creative expression, the phenomenon of the institutionalizing of art--the arbitrary standard that accords the oil painting status, but not the *ververs*, that honors the written novel, but not the oral narrative, and accepts the piano, but not steel drums. Through artist figures in his novels, Lamming illustrates the tightrope that the artist must walk in his interaction with politics: "I think that one of the best political contributions . . . [the artist] can make to the society is to write good books," says Lamming, adding, "I do not share the notion of the artist being the private person withdrawn from society."[17] appears, then, to see the artist, like Chiki, working for social renewal behind the protective mask of fiction but at the same time abhorring violence and eschewing direct political involvement. He calls for a revolution, but one that will transform the individual's approach to reality, provoking the interchange of dialogue rather than the domination by arbitrarily imposed assumptions.

Chiki is only one manifestation of Lamming's employment of the trickster as artistic re-former. For the spirit of Anancy is very much present in *Castle of My Skin*. Features of the trickster, we will recall, are his role as scapegoat; his involvement at points of social change and exchange; his creative energy, symbolized by his inordinately long phallus (Legba) or his weaving skill (Anancy);[18] his handling of dung (representing taboo items) which be converts into wisdom and healing "medicine" for the tribe; and his affinity for paradox and ambiguity which leads him repeatedly to confound partial and arbitrary assumptions.

The physical landscape of *In the Castle of My Skin* expresses a hierarchical structuring of society that seems fixed and permanent. Boundaries formed by walls and partitions abound. High on the hill are the landlord's house and garden surrounded by a brick wall topped with broken glass, while below in the valley is the "tenantry"--the folk defined in terms of their relationship to the landlord: "At night the light poured down through the wood, and the house looking down from the hill seemed to hold a quality of benevolent protection. It was a castle around which the land like a shabby back garden stretched" (p. 29). The gracious living that marks this house and walled garden is on another plane of reality from the life of villagers, who observe activities of "the Great" in open-mouthed awe.

Another walled enclosure on the landscape of *In the Castle of My Skin* is the school yard with its "three shrines of enlightenment that looked over the wall and across a benighted wooden tenantry" (p. 35). The three "shrines" are the church with "dark stained hooded windows that never opened" (p. 35) and an interior that is "dark and heavy and strange" (p. 35); the head teacher's house; and the school itself "with windows all around that opened like a yawning mouth" (p. 35). It is not without significance that a language of sacredness is used for this structured landscape in which religion puts a veil over the eyes of the folk, while the school turns village children into fodder for the system. Imprisoned within these walls of imposed cultural values are the folk, as anachronistic within the dominant system as the flourishing palm tree in the fourth corner of the yard.

The landscaped village with its lighted Great House on the hill overseeing the tenantry in the valley and the sacred middle ground between them of religion and education is a microcosm of the novel's larger landscape in which Big England and Little England coexist in the parent-child relationship typical of colonialism. The landscape of colonialism, of "enlightened" civilization and benighted outsiders, is the very scene of *Castle*'s action. "Landlords" of authority--England, the Great House, the school, the church--all "look down" across their boundary walls at a "tenantry" beyond.

The great protect their own interests by means of a system of overseers, supervisors, and inspectors, but the folk, by contrast, are without protection; they experience invasion of their fragile defining boundaries at every point. The frail walls of the village suggest a corresponding frailty of the walls of personhood for those who live there: "The village was a marvel of small, heaped houses raised jauntily on groundsels of limestone, and arranged in rows on either side of the multiplying marl roads. Sometimes the roads disintegrated, the limestone slid back and the houses advanced across their boundaries in an embrace of board and shingle and cactus fence" (p. 10). An initial reading leads to the conclusion that the villagers lack a clearly marked "road" of purpose. Defined by others, they are yet to define themselves. Their ill-defined selfhood, their constant experience of being "overseen," is symbolized in the incident of G's bath time. As the neighbor's son Bob balances on the paling to watch, his weight causes a fence to crash: "the two yards merged. The barricade which had once protected our [the narrator's] private secrecies had surrendered" (p. 18). A crowd is attracted to the scene:

On all sides the fences had been weighed down with people, boys and girls and grown-ups. The girls were laughing and looking across to where I stood on the pool of pebbles, naked, waiting. They looked at Bob's mother and the broken fence and me. The sun had dried me thoroughly, and now it seemed that I had not been bathed, but brought out in open condemnation and placed in the middle of the yard waiting like one crucified to be jeered at. (p. 19)

The scene recurs in different forms throughout the novel: shame and degradation consequent on the breaking down of defining boundaries, ritual beatings, ritual purifications. Mocking eyes rejoice over the trembling naked figure of another's embarrassment, glad to find a scapegoat for the shame they fear to confront within themselves. G's naked skin is his sole protection--his frail counterpart to the landlord's "castle" on the hill.

Boundary walls define the Great, then, but merely marginalize the folk, categorizing them as expiatory scapegoats for the Great. G and his friends transgress sacred boundaries when they secretly enter the grounds of the landlord's house to see what goes on at a party. There they witness the seduction of the landlord's daughter by a British sailor, but the story later given out by the landlord is that his daughter was raped by the village boys. Here the "penetration" of sacred domains--the rape of class interests by the military--is projected onto the folk. Similarly, moral corruption within the ranks of those bonded together by a common "skin" is denied. Moral and economic problems are univocally displaced into simple racial hatred. Villagers conversing in the shoemaker's shop sum up the landlord's relationship with the folk with more acuity than they realize when one of them says, "He couldn't feel as happy anywhere else in this God's world than he feel on that said same hill lookin' down at us" (p. 97).

Just as the landlord lays his sin on the sacrificial scapegoat of the collective folk, so the folk themselves repeat the performance. Wilson Harris has pointed to the ritual beatings and washing ceremonies in *Castle*.[19] When her pumpkin vine is trampled, G's mother has a sense of loss and futility that is wider-reaching than the immediate waste of the plant. Her voice "spoke as if from an inner void beyond which deeper within herself were incalculable layers of feeling" (p. 17). Her deprivation vents itself on G. The boy, completely innocent, stands naked in the center of a circle of spectators who rock with laughter as his mother engages in a ritualistic beating. Her injunction "Don't move . . . if you move I lash you," and G's escape maneuvers join them in a "game of cat and mouse" (p. 19) that seems more concerned with gratifying the needs of beater and spectator than with a just correction of behavior. Shame is felt, a scapegoat is needed, and the naked boy serves the role. Each needs the darkness of another so that he can deny the darkness within himself.

Projection of guilt and shame onto an innocent victim occurs again in an incident involving the Head teacher of the village school. The occasion is the Queen's birthday, and a visit from the school inspector. Squads of boys are drawn up in formation in the school yard--a spectacle tellingly described from the mature viewpoint of the older G as "an enormous ship whose cargo had been packed in boxes and set on the deck" (p. 36). Colonial education is depicted as a subtle form of slavery whose goal appears to be emulation of the Great--correct "performance" achieved by memorization, voice control, and generally keeping in step. At no point are opinions asked or inquiry encouraged, and local event and history are irrelevant. When the ceremony is interrupted by a loud giggle, the head teacher's response is dramatic. On the departure of the inspector he addresses the school in a voice "choked with a kind of terror" (p. 42). Punishment falls on the first available victim in ritualistic sadism: the innocent lad becomes "a human symbol of the blackest sin," is bound hand and foot and a leather strap brought down repeatedly on his buttocks until his clothing is ripped and the "filth slithered down his legs." Like a sacrificial victim, the boy "made a brief howl like an animal that had had its throat cut" (p. 43). Asked why he didn't run, the boy replied, "He had to beat somebody, and he made sure with me" (p. 43). Like the men in Foster's shop, the boy understands the human need for a scapegoat. As his school friends bathe away the filth and blood, the victim relates information about the head teacher that fully explains the man's insecurities and his need to protect his image at all costs.

The same performance occurs even in the name of Christianity. At the wayside service a circle forms once again around the boy, "naked in sin" (p. 162), who is destined, as G understands, to be a "sacrifice" (p. 162). Again the pattern is of the authority figure humiliating and denigrating a victim while the circle of worshipers and spectators exult in projecting their own shame. As the ceremony comes to an end, the candlelight goes out, recalling for us Boy Blue's habitual response to teasing about his black skin: "Just as I was goin' to born the light went out." Recontextualized here, Boy Blue's words take on a new and solemn meaning. Boy Blue accepts his own blackness, his identity; in contrast, the symbolically nameless boy, by accepting the darkness of others projected onto himself, becomes "a prisoner in the light" (p. 163). Here, as in a variety of ways throughout the novel, Lamming inverts the conventional Christian usage of light as a positive and dark as a negative symbol. To embrace the darkness, in Lamming's universe, is the only way to self-knowledge and the freedom it brings.

Lamming's key metaphor for the invasion of boundaries and absence of defining walls of selfhood is the flood with which the novel opens. Water seeps through ceiling and floor into the house where G lives with his mother. Outside, a lily is uprooted from the soil by the force of the rain. Invading floodwaters anticipate the later "flood" of worker riots that will invade the boundaries of privilege but leave in their wake a muddy residue of bourgeois profiteering personified in Mr. Slime, founder of the Penny Bank--an organization that, despite its promise, yields no benefits to the village. At an existential level the floodwaters provide an image for the novel's exploration of ways to build defining walls around the self. For repeatedly the self experiences invasion by the other: "Deep down he felt uneasy. He had been seen by another. He had become part of the other's world, and therefore no longer in complete control of his own. The eye of another was a kind of cage" (p. 73). Release and freedom are found only in the darkness--in the darkened cinema, in the school lavatory. G searches for means to exchange imprisonment within the perceiving eye of another person for a "castle" of the self that defies invasion. He is contending, of course, with the existential paradox that retreat to the darkness outside of the perception (*le regard*) of the other is a movement into nonbeing, while to be defined by the other is to be misconceived--a similar state of nonbeing.

Lamming takes his title from a couplet of Walcott's "Juvenilia":

You in the castle of your skin
I the swineherd.[20]

The conventional romance situation, invoked here by Walcott, of unattainable mistress and infatuated, self-denigrating admirer (fine picture of the imitation of the Great in the colonial situation) is ironically inverted throughout the novel. The folk figure, at the beginning of the novel, is found in a "shabby back garden" *outside* the "castle" of privilege, but at its conclusion is *inside* an impregnable castle of his own--the castle of his "skin." G discovers how to avoid being "defined" by another. Grinning behind his mask, he declares, "The likenesses will meet and make merry, but they won't know you, the you that's hidden somewhere in the castle of your skin" (p. 261). His mask frees him from the cage of the perceiving eye; acceptance of his darkness brings freedom. Enacted against a backcloth of worker riots that will ultimately lead to national independence, G's drama is an existential taking possession of the boundaries of the self; he converts the cage of the already defined into the fortress of the ever signifying.

G, in fact, discovers the power that resides in the margins of structure--power that is symbolized in trickster lore by phallic imagery. When the trickster converts dung into "medicine," he attributes creative energy to that which social structure rejects. Appropriately, since the novel at its realistic level deals with the maturation process of a young lad, sexuality is pervasive. The small boys who play with pins on the railway tracks look forward to the time when their "small blades" will be exchanged for the real weapons that the bigger boys display. Crabs, dogs, frogs, humans--all copulate in the regions beyond the village. The phallus is omnipresent.

Yet castration, too, is evident as the folk are identified with a broken phallus. Discovery of their sexual potential by the boys in the bath is checked and punished by the supervisor. Insistence on monogamy creates havoc for Jon and Bambi, producing a dilemma in which any attempt at choice (the means of self-definition) becomes autocastration. Religion, too, plays its part, exhorting youths to be "born again" at the moment when nascent manhood demands they accept responsibility for themselves. Trumper describes a man who refuses to be involved in the process of political decision making--preferring to be defined by others--as being like "a monk with a rotten cock who ain't know how he come by the said same infirmity" (p. 293).

The broken phallus motif is supported by the story line. G begins from a point of deprivation, "an almost total absence of family relations" (p. 12), and a past that has sunk "with its cargo of episodes like a crew preferring scuttle to the consequences of survival" (p. 11). Like his past and present, the boy's future, too, with his fears and ideals, seems destined to go down the drain in the same way as the flood waters that have washed out his ninth birthday (p. 10). Subsequent events bring only greater deprivation. Like the uprooted lily in the flood, G will be removed from the village to attend high school, and the novel will end on the point of his departure for Trinidad at the age of nineteen. Uprooting, deprivation, discontinuity, absence of relationships, painful loss--these characterize his forward movement in time.

Behind him the villagers' experience echoes his own. Any hope for improvement of their lot through assumption of political or economic power seems destined to fail. Slime's Penny Bank scheme and the workers' riots alike seem to leave the folk rather worse off than they were under the landlord's feudal overlordship. Mr. Foster, who realizes that "a man ain't a man till he can call the house he live in my own" (p. 240), has become a legend in the village for clinging tenaciously to his house. When floodwaters lifted it off its groundsels, he launched it downstream like a new Noah's ark. Yet he is dispossessed by Slime's organization. The novel closes on the demolition of Foster's home and the removal of Pa from *his* family house to the almshouse. Exploitation and dispossession are the story of the folk--under slavery, under the colonial landlord, and now under the emergent national bourgeoisie. James Ngugi suggests that Lamming's solution--the "united struggle of dispossessed"--is communicated by Trumper in *Castle*:[21] "'You think they dare move all these houses,' he asked. 'If all o' you decide to sleep in the street or let the Government find room for you in the prison house, you think they dare go through with this business o' selling the land?'" (p. 286). It would seem, though, that to take Trumper's words as Lamming's final statement is to embrace an oversimplification that G himself is chary of. The inadequacy of the racial ideology

Trumper declaims is exposed ironically by juxtaposition of event in the text. For even as Trumper enthuses over his newly found sense of racial identity, black bourgeois politics is moving in to dispossess Foster and Pa.

Just as the story is of brokenness and fragmentation, so is the plot. Depending entirely on chronology for its unity, the plot discovers little meaning or purpose in either G's story or that of the community. Mimesis fails to provide the connections or relationships that will give signification to events. Meaning lies beyond the annals of history, as Trumper says: "Don't ask Hist'ry why you is what you then see yourself to be, 'cause Hist'ry ain't got no answers. You ain't a thing till you know it" (p. 297).

Yet, though the forward movement of the novel is pessimistic, though imitation leads to ignominious failure and mimesis fails to uncover meaning--though, in a word, read as a conventional bildungsroman, Lamming's *In the Castle of My Skin* seems almost without hope--there is an alternative way of interpreting the text that emphasizes not hopeless sequence, but connection. Lamming's "grotesque" scrap bag of incidents, anecdotes, and descriptions is, in fact, a tricksterlike assembling of the dismembered god. Like a novitiate contemplating the sacra of the tribe, the reader must consider the connections between parts, the relationships that give meaning. In such a strategic rereading, the village landscape signifies an alternative ideology. Its disintegrating road, the "embrace of board and shingle and cactus fence," and houses advancing "across their boundaries to meet those on the opposite side" (p. 10), speak eloquently of a universe of relationships, of connections, of wholeness set over against the divisive structures that dominate.

For Lamming does not give us G's diary--but a novel, a rereading of the diary, interspersed with anecdote and folktale. His text is not history, but a web of signification relating one fragment to another. The G who writes the narrative is other than the G who is contained in the text. G as textual character is not, like the trickster-artist, able to use his perspective of distance (temporally and spatially removed from events) to weave threads into new configurations. The trickster-artist at the interstices where juxtaposed fragments reflect upon each other, however, can divine significance: the spider's web is a "system of signs."

The process of stepping outside a containing metaphor of life into a position from which one can survey oneself in ironic appraisal is latent in the maturation process as described by French psychologist Jean Piaget. Piaget identifies four stages in the development of the child, which shed light on our discussion of the adult G's exile.[22] The stages are as follows:

Age	*Stage*
Birth to 18 months	sensorimotor (prespeech)
18 months to 7-8 years	representation (postspeech but preoperatory)
7-12 years	concrete operations
12 years onwards	propositional/formal operations

Until 18 months, Piaget argues, the child lives in an "egocentric space," and the objective world exists for him only as his senses record it. Later he moves to "general space," and is aware of all objects, including his own body, as existing in that general space. This "total decentration in relation to the original egocentricspace" Piaget describes as a "Copernican revolution."[23] The point here is that the infant is contained in reality, yet is unaware of being so contained. The advent of speech accompanies his movement outside himself, providing, as it were, the ability to represent himself to himself. From 7-12 years of age, he apprehends reality through concrete metaphor, but not until he approaches 12 years is he able to reason in the abstract, weighing one proposition against another--standing outside his metaphors in ironic contemplation.

It is surely of profound significance that Piaget identifies the acquisition of speech as that factor which permits the step outside of egocentrism into awareness of a world-space peopled with otherness. As the child represents his world in language, he is exiled from that world into the inner space of his mind, from which he contemplates not only his world but his own being. But the later stage of growth is more remarkable still: the child now retreats into the exile of hypothesis in order to comment critically and ironically on his own mental landscape: his own thought is divided against itself. Representational thought, in a word, is critiqued by the more integrative processes of imagination. The boys in Lamming's first novel discuss the power of speech and the control and release it brings. Of still deeper significance, though, is the formal device that replaces G the chronicler with G the mythmaker. G leaps out of representational modes into the paradoxes and ambiguities of an ironic vision.

Thus the difference between G within the text and G who narrates is akin to the difference between the prespeech and the representational stages of childhood, or the difference between concrete and formal operation. In the first case, the child can move outside reality and represent it by words, but it is only in the later stage that ambiguity is possible. Juxtaposing the paradoxical and contradictory, the mind proceeds from the

known (concrete) to the unknown, and this, in essence, conditions
creative potential. In each case, the movement out of reality into
a reflective mode permits new dimensions of maturity. In the
later stage, paradox becomes the ground for invention.

Unless he represents himself to himself, unless, in addition, he
can stand in exile outside structure and embrace paradox and
ambiguity, the child fails to develop. Returning to *Castle*, we
could draw the parallel that merely to exist in time is not enough,
nor is a mere historical representation of events sufficient. Time
moves in one direction through the novel, but counter to that
flow is the reflective movement of memory, of the mature G
narrating the fragments of his life, revising, reversing, juxtaposing to provide the relationships that reveal meaning. In this
reflective movement, contradictions and paradox are held in
skillful balance.

The twin movement--forward in time and backward in
revisionist reflection--are captured in the early pages of the novel
in a passage that will serve here as introduction to our discussion
of the place of written narrative as self-creation: "The clock
shelved in one corner kept up its ticking. My mother retreated to
another part of the house where the silk and taffeta designs of
her needling were being revised and reversed. I soon followed"
(p. 12).

At many points in G's narrative, the historical line is abandoned, and a timeless moment of harmony and pattern shapes
itself as the people group together at the telling and hearing of
tales. One such moment occurs as G's mother, Miss Foster, and
Bob's mother gather. Harmony, meaning, and fecundity take the
place of deprivation and loss as the women recreate their world:

> They sat in the shade under the cherry tree that spread out
> over the fences in all directions. The roots were in one yard,
> but its body bulged forth into another, and its branches struck
> out over three or four more .... They sat in a circle composed
> and relaxed, rehearsing, each in turn, the tale of dereliction
> told a thousand times during the past week .... It seemed they
> were three pieces in a pattern which remained constant .... In
> the corner where one fence merged into another, and the
> sunlight filtering through the leaves made a limitless suffusion
> over the land, the pattern had arranged itself with absolute
> unawareness .... The three were shuffling episodes and
> exchanging the confidences which informed their life with
> meaning. (pp. 24-25)

The full meaning, however, is not clear to the women. As the
narrator explains, "Their consciousness had never been quickened
by the fact of life to which these confidences might have been
a sure testimony" (p. 25). For greater self-awareness there must

be a further distancing. It is only when Trumper leaves the island that he is able to see with any degree of clarity what it means to be a Negro and to "proclaim himself the blackest evidence of the white man's denial of conscience" (p. 299). Similarly, G perceives that, painful as it is, withdrawal into a noman's-land of exile--outside history, outside the defining relationships of society--alone makes possible gnosis. In fact, Lamming transforms the negativity of dispossession--which finds its ultimate expression in exile--into a positive ground of self-knowledge. It is the mature narrator, from his perspective in exile from the folk he reflects on, who infuses into the fragmented life of the village the existential overtones, the significant juxtapositions, and the key words evoking rich associative links, thus injecting meaning where linear narrative yields only purposelessness and despair.

Situated within history, G is limited by the Puritan frame of perception that determines and prefigures all he sees. Both his own tone and that of others of the folk is often condemnatory: the boys are "vagabonds," "disrespectful varmints," "hooligans," and "grinning jackasses." The natural world beyond the boundaries of social structure teems with life, but it is described in morally derogatory terms. There is a awed revulsion before forces that are seemingly both powerful and dangerous. In the woods, an old woman stumbles on copulating dogs "shaggy and obscene in their excitement," and human couples "gross and warm in frenzied intercourse" (p. 33). The boys observe the couplings of crabs on the beach and are "fascinated and terrified" in the woods by the ferocity of mating cats and the "hideous posture" (p. 171) assumed by a pair of frogs. Their revulsion at this country on the margins, a landscape that defies and threatens their sense of order and structure (they are, we recall, adolescents), is rendered tangible in the viscous "ooze-like jelly" from the mating frogs into which Trumper inadvertently puts his hand. Conditioned by a Puritanical society, they consider the natural, the sexual, the procreative as a nasty and distasteful business.

But this is the attitude of youthful immaturity. Despite the mental castration suggested in their reactions, a current of laughter surges through the novel, celebrating sexuality, denying responsibility, and revealing the locus of corruption not in the marginalized folk and their nature, but in the very center of authority's sacred constructs. This laughter is the sure manifestation of the trickster. It is fully and pervasively evident in the tales and anecdotes related by the folk in Castle. For every repressive statement or edict made by authority, there is a counterstatement made by the folk, inverting, parodying, punning, and generally laying bare the hollow sham at the core of all authoritarian assertion.

A fine example is the story of Jon. Western authoritarian

standards enter Jon's life when he runs into the "free-for-all Brethren." Deliciously misinterpreting this nomenclature, he freely takes Brother Bannister's daughter for himself and impregnates the girl. Required by the good churchman (at gun point) to marry the young lady, lest shame come on both church and Brother Bannister himself, Jon is faced with the problem of Susie, the mother of his children. Jon's solution is to agree to marry both girls, but on the appointed day he sits in a tree in the churchyard, choosing neither, while the two congregations wait in vain.

On the surface the story reads like a disruption of rural mores by an intrusive religious code. Jon seems helpless in his vacillation--castrated in his inability to make a mature choice. There is, however, a key to an alternative "reading"--the three-times-repeated phrase "like a feather in the wind." Jon finds himself outside of structure, threatened on one hand by Bannister with his gun, representing European values, and on the other by Susie with her bottle of arsenic, representing the folk institution. "Poor Jon was betwix' the devil an' the deep blue sea," Trumper comments. But Jon chooses to make liminality his strength. Refusing to shift from his ambiguous position, he assumes the role of trickster. Symbolically positioning himself up a tree in the cemetery--suspended between heaven and earth, life and death--he waits for the hater of contradictions to contradict himself. "He stay there quiet as a mouse an' he see all the commotion, an' he hear all what they was sayin' 'bout where he wus, an' he just look an' listen" (p. 125). And his wait is rewarded, as the priest and Brother Bannister reveal, in their angry interchange, a great deal that they should have preferred to have kept hidden. Trumper captures the glee of the trickster in his words: "I never know there wus so much to tell 'bout the clergy, an' only God in heaven knows if it's all true, but we here in this earth can only hope it ain't true, the things I hear about the clergy" (p. 125). From his liminal position, Jon thus provokes an "exchange" that frees him from the power of assumed authority, exposing the sacred assumptions of a dominant, repressive culture to reexamination, if not ridicule, while skillfully evading all responsibility himself (a denial of responsibility repeated in the narrative strategy of using the child-mask of Trumper to recount the tale). The triumph of the trickster's phallus is exuberantly celebrated by Trumper: "Some say this, an' some say that, but no matter what some say or not say, everybody start to refer to Jon as the cock of the yard. An' some say cocks wus gettin' scarce. What a scandal it wus, an' I hear things about cocks I never hear in all my born days. 'Twus a hell of a mix-up, an' I hope never to hear of such a thing again" (p. 124).

Another tale about "cocks" is related by Miss Foster; it is the incident of Gordon's "mannishness" in attempting to enter the white man's world of economics by selling a fowl cock (and ah, how intentional is the pun!) to a white man standing at the bus stop. As Gordon turns the fowl around, the expected happens. The bird messes in the man's face. Gleefully, the boys relate to an investigating police officer how the man fled because he had messed his pants, while children around tease him with a song, "Look what fowlcock do to you."

Responsibility for the incident lies, of course, with the fowl cock--not with Gordon.[24] Wearing a mask of childlike innocence, he initiates an "exchange" that will expose the shame of the authority figure--the white man, who throws coins for the boys to dive for, hands out pennies on public occasions, but denies economic independence to the folk he exploits.

And so, despite repression and attempted castration, the phallus of the trickster is omnipresent. Outside the margins of history, trickster reassembles his fragmented phallus: he draws together meaningless threads of experience, and so creates a web that ensnares his prey in its sticky meshes. Trumper describes his own experience of such a creative moment: "I wus sittin' under the cellar at home, I don't remember why I went under the cellar, p'raps I wus searching for eggs. But anyhow, I wus there, under the cellar, an' it seem I wus all by myself there under the cellar, jus' looking at the dust and dirt an' rubbish under the cellar" (p. 122). The whole world, so an African creation story tells us, was born from an egg. It is under the cellar, removed to the margins of the house, that Trumper begins the process of creating his world anew.

In the same way as Trumper, G salvages his life from the rubbish. Looking at his diaries, he realizes that, like the "cargo of episodes" on the scuttled ship of his family past, the records of his own past are destined to be "put away on the shelf and . . . never heard of again except someone rescues them from the garbage" (p. 258). That is, unless they are reread and revised as they are in the novel itself. The written word, as Derrida points out, is infinitely iterable, renewing its life constantly through repeated recontextualizations that are independent of the author, indeed that are premised upon his absence. For the author is indeed "absent." He is neither the G within the text nor the G who narrates, but someone else, somewhere else. Thus the notion of exile creates ever-widening ripples of signification. The Anancy artist, then, escapes oblivion by means of his thread--the narrative thread spun from his own historical being. He draws the single spun thread into a multiplicity of relationships and configurations that reveal his divining powers--his ability to search between events for the meaning that lies in the interstices. The novel's discussion of "getting into history" is thus resolved in the act of artistic creation.

For all attempts at climbing into history ultimately fail. Man does not define himself by epic heroism: the big fisherman on the beach is a man only when he ceases to be godlike. Nor is a man made by his actions, since "stoning" either headmaster or landlord results only in the replacement of one authority by another. Assuming the responsibility of choice, too, is meaningless in a society that does not offer valid choices. Self-definition, as Lamming describes it, is not measured by material gain, and, indeed, is not achieved *in time*. It consists, instead, in reflection, in stepping outside time into inner spaces of the imagination.

One aspect of the trickster remains to be discussed: his handling of dung, which he converts into "medicine" for the tribe. On the way home from a farewell party held in honor of his departure for Trinidad, G is intercepted by a prostitute. At the party he was "cock in the yard"; now he has the opportunity to "prove" his manhood in the time-honored way. But he chooses instead to tell the girl a story. The tale in full reads as follows:

> When I was a little boy I knew another little boy who was in the habit of accumulating birds' shit. When he got the right quantity he cut a stick and painted it with the birds' shit. He hid the stick till it was dark, and when he went out, unseen and hardly seeing, he would make conversation with another boy. Then he would ask the boy to hold the stick, and when the boy held he pulled the stick through the clenched fingers, and the paint came off in a solid little pile on the other's hand. She said it was very, very funny, but she didn't understand why I told her. I couldn't wait to explain. (p. 261)

The boy in the story epitomizes the impulse to project one's darkness onto another, to use another's humiliation and shame to prove one's own manhood. Unwittingly the prostitute is acquiescing in this process, allowing her body to become a "hide of darkness" (to use Brathwaite's phrase) for another's guilt.[25] G refuses to win "manhood" so cheaply.

Like the boy, the trickster-artist takes the accumulated "shit"--the shame of the folk--and (like G, who appropriates his childhood acquaintance's scatology for his own storied didacticism) converts it, through the ritual of his text, into "medicine." Healing is made possible through the trickster-artist's exposure of the process by which human beings, black and white alike, project their own shame onto others and refuse to confront their inner darkness. The discovery that the shameful, defiling "shit" is, in reality, the "blackest evidence" of another's denial of conscience, gives wisdom and power, as Trumper has realized.

And so, like the spider-trickster, G leaves society, retreating into the margins to spin his web. He goes--where else?--to Trinidad. His mother expresses her disgust at "that kind o' playing hooligan ... like wild cats ... as if some demon inside them get away" (p. 271). But G is simply "dying" to experience--carnival!

The carnivalesque figures prominently in Harris's work, too, though admittedly less overtly than in the example of G's journey beyond the boundaries of his childhood world to participate in carnival in Trinidad. My contention is that Harris's technique, too, is that of the trickster-artist. He insists on ambiguity (making rich use of puns to explore the multivocality of the word); he privileges metaphor and image over sequential linearity of event (plot line) and factual representation of character and place; and he engages in a narrative strategy that provides a reflective rereading of events as they are unfolding. The novel chosen to illustrate this trickster strategy is *Genesis of the Clowns* (1977). This novel, which takes the form of a correspondence, is a dialogue between past and present, between historic and mythic points of view, between narrator and characters, and between author and reader.

From within the text of *Genesis of the Clowns*, I wish to concentrate on the figure of the trickster as it appears in a particular pairing of complementary characters: Chung and Hope. In these two men Harris explores what he calls the limbo-Anancy syndrome. Limbo dancing and the telling of Anancy stories are both aspects of a folk response to the deprivation consequent on the middle passage journey. Drawing on these expressions of folk creativity, Harris develops an art of the dispossessed. Like the limbo dancer, and like Anancy the spider, he creates a world of relationships where formerly there existed a void between oppressive structures.

Before expanding the analysis of the present discussion by focusing on *Genesis of the Clowns*, it is wise to survey first what Harris says about the artist as Anancy. In an interview with John Thieme in by *Caribbean Contact*, Harris discusses a creative alternative to the human impulse of domination and consolidation of sovereign premises.[26] We live, Harris says, in an "asymmetrical cosmos" in which there can be no place for fixed assumptions, only an ongoing creative response to change--disastrous though the relinquishing of our constructs may seem. He concedes the possible existence of an ultimate reality but argues that our perceptions of reality are only partial: "the ground of reality in an absolutely ultimate sense may be changeless, but it remains for us something which is unnameable, something which cannot be structured." Harris proposes that the proper approach to the "unnameable centre," the unfathomable wholeness of reality, is metaphor--for the reality lies always *between* our constructs. He explains as follows: "When one says, for example, the sun is a rose, one is involved . . . in an unnameable centre of light that exists between the sun and the rose." Metaphor, then, for Harris, is "not an ornament . . . not a conceit.

Built into it is a sensation that all images witness to a reality that
is ceaselessly deeper than the very moorings from which they
originally sprang." From this premise Harris argues for a
redefinition of tradition, suggesting that tradition lies in "the
search for cross-cultural connections." His argument continues
with the notion that buried or underground cultures, as alterna-
tives to existing structures, must be unearthed if one is to recover
the "light" that exists always between, never within, our concepts.
Consequently, the reappearance of such cultures is "essential if
one is genuinely to come into some ground of authority which
would make freedom a reality." Even language itself is subject
to interstitial investigation since it is "never perfectly transpar-
ent, but ... can carry within it layers of illumination that mutate
and come to the surface," with the result that "a work of the
imagination has a strange life which goes far deeper than the
historical framework or decade in which it is set." In sum, Harris
stresses the importance of interstices, of silences, of buried
resources, as a saving restraint on the consolidation of dominant
structures which, though they claim total sovereignty and
absolute authority, are always partial. The word, or light, is to
be found neither in Western ideology nor in the "buried" cultures
of the Caribbean, but in the meeting of the two, in a "collision"
of cultures.

The artist, in Harris's thought, becomes the mediator between
buried resources and partial constructs, trekking shamanlike into
the wilderness beyond structure to confront society with the
silent witness of what it has overlooked. Such continual confrontation with the other he sees as the only hope for existence in a
changing cosmos. The meeting point of cultures, of ideologies, is,
then, the point of both danger and power, and the artist stands
tricksterlike, in limbo, in the gateway, or on the threshold to a
new world.

Harris discusses this limbo experience in his essay "History,
Fable, and Myth in the Caribbean and the Guianas."[27] Here he
conflates the limbo dance with Haitian vodun. Evoking through
puns the notion of the dismembered god (phantom limb/limbo)
and the experience of loss, of having fallen into the interstices
between two worlds (void/vodun), Harris describes an "art of the
dispossessed" manifest in West Indian folk forms. It is this
capacity for "arts of originality springing out of an age of limbo"
that marks a true creative phenomenon in the West Indies, Harris
argues. The accommodation of forms drawn from both old and
new worlds of experience within a limbo-void of deprivation is
itself evidence of creativity--creativity that leads away from
destructive polarizations. This "ground of accommodation, this
art of creative coexistence, pointing away from apartheid and
ghetto fixations, is of the utmost importance and *native* to the
Caribbean." The "ground of accommodation" is represented by

limbo dancers themselves, some of whom dance godlike on high stilts, while others move close to the ground ("spider-anancy masks" Harris calls them) invoking "a curious reassembly of the parts of the dead god or gods." Harris's "reading" of vodun trance dances similarly stresses relationships rather than separate entities. The dancers, in his description, lose their initial self-possession and become objects within a spatial dimension of relationships. The dancers themselves, however, may remain unenlightened by the vision "articulated in their involuntary theme"; the writer, on the other hand, in visualizing his "drama of consciousness," experiences "a slow revelation or unraveling of obscurity." To Harris, the written word mediates between unconscious symbolic gesture and the perceiving consciousness. He thus defines the writer as interpreter of inarticulated experience. It is interesting to note that both Harris and Lamming see the writer in this complementary relationship with the folk; while a certain inarticulateness characterizes the drums of *Season* and the dancer in Harris's "History, Fable, and Myth," the writer, using the ever-changing structures and masks of words and metaphor, raises and deepens the unstructured consciousness communicated in folktale and ritual. As Harris puts it, "The community the writer shares with the primordial dancer is, as it were, the complementary halves of a broken stage." The novelist, then, in Harris's description, brings the antistructure of folk experience, expressed symbolically in ritual, into the structured form of written texts--texts, though, that are "texts" (weavings) indeed, polylogic texts that invite a multiplicity of readings.

In sum, then, assuming the inaccessibility of any transcendent signified, Harris stresses the importance of relationships between constructs rather than the constructs themselves, and the un-restricted play of signifiers, none of which is privileged above another. He accords metaphor as much authority as factual statement, and researches the "apparently irrelevant" yet "curious footnotes in the history books" that, he claims, "sometimes speak volumes."[28] Contextualizing his argument in the Caribbean experience, he describes the limbo or void of interstitiality inhabited by a folk caught between two cultures and illustrates that creativity lies in the capacity to draw together the fragments of shattered certainties--broken gods--into new formal relation-ships. Creativity is thus conceived as a continuing capacity to enter the void beyond structure in order to accommodate and embrace new, contradictory, and initially disorienting experience. We have seen how the limbo dance is "read" by Harris as such an art of accommodation. In his novel *Genesis of the Clowns*, Harris uses limbo imagery to depict folk response to interstitiality. Grounding his text in folk ritual in this way, Harris demonstrates his assertion that the artist articulates in words what the folk express in nonverbal gesture.

The narrator of *Genesis of the Clowns*, Frank Wellington, an ex-surveyor now living in London, is prompted by a letter informing him of the death in Guyana of a former colleague, Hope, to reminisce on his days in the Guyana hinterland. Receipt of the letter initiates a journey in memory that takes the narrator out of the time and space he exists in historically into a liminal "midsummer day's dream" (p. 81) in which all conventional boundaries are collapsed: the past enters the present and the present reflects on the past in a reciprocal transformation and translation.

Genesis, as both its title and subtitle (*A Comedy of Light*) suggest, is a creation myth. Frank Wellington, surveyor turned artist, leaves the epic measuring and possessing of the material landscape in an attempt to return, through reflective discourse, to a myth of origins and a spiritual survey. Instead of carving up the land--charting, measuring, and dividing--Wellington now enters into a correspondence (Heidegger's co-respondence)[29] with a reality lying buried within the "landscape" he had formerly charted, and to a hidden self buried within each of the men who came to his table for monetary payment in the past, but who now come for a different, nonmaterial evaluation of their worth. As the trickster-artist seated at the table of "exchange" returns, in dream, to the text of his field book, he finds the footnotes and marginalia more revealing than the factual record. "History," muses Frank Wellington's correspondent, "may possess an unwritten anecdote, an eclipsed but naked spiritual fact" (p. 146). Wellington's search, like Harris's, takes him in a movement counter to historical progress, backwards into mythic revision. The artist engaged in rewriting reality in a way that deconstructs the text of his surveyor's field book, is, in the terms of this discussion, the figure of Anancy--lover of paradox and contradiction, dwelling in the margins, and revealing the tragic limitations of the House built by authority, Mr. Hate-to-Be-Contradicted.

Thus the dual movement of the novel--its chronological flow countered by a revisionary reading--is an embrace of paradox and ambiguity; it is the "facing both ways in perpetual ambiguity" characteristic of the trickster. And since, as Harris has intimated, it is metaphor that allows us to slip between the oppressive structures of empirical thought into a marginal space where creative thought can restructure the world, it follows that metaphor is prominent in Harris's work. A complex mesh of images enriches--rather, is the very fabric of--*Genesis of the Clowns*. The gun that appears to threaten destruction at various points in the narrative is also a phallus, capable of loving intercourse and impregnation as well as of rape; rivets (recontextualized from Conrad's *Heart of Darkness*)--"obsessed rivets of blood" (p. 84), "myself riveted into a breathless tapestry of continents" (p. 86)--are discovered to be mere "rivets of pollen"

(p. 93), the fertile promise of new life. Movement is stillness, and stillness is dance in the planetry, cosmic images of the novel: the globe we stand on "stands still as it turns around a central darkness of buried sun to create an illusion of dual immobility, revolution within counter- revolution, as the arrested whirlpool of light" (p. 45). And in this Hegelian reading of the cosmos, silence itself is "the arrested momentum of speech" (p. 44). Over and over again the imagery defies the univocality of structuring perception, laying bare contradictions within the reality we only think we perceive. In a key image, Harris draws attention to the contrary movement of surface and depths in the Abary River, caused by tidal waters from the Atlantic:

> A faculty existed in the Atlantic for inflowing tides from the ocean to persist in the Abary river much longer than one dreamt when the surface of the river itself had already turned with outflowing strength. We detected this with floats submerged at certain depths. Each float carried its flag above the surface of the river and when suddenly these began to move against the stream, like the hand of myth, one was aware not only of wheels within wheels but of revolutions turning in opposite and contrary directions. (p. 87)

On the one hand, a dimension of conquest is invoked through the territorial markers--the flags--and, on the other, the revolutionary movement of submerged forces. The countermovement is "like the hand of myth"--a phrase crucial to the passage, directing the reader to Harris's mythic mode that flows in the opposite direction to the tide of historical development or conventional plot line. His is an "inverse craft" (to use a phrase from *Palace of the Peacock*) a reflective discourse, mirroring the past through the memory of the folk, the memory of landscape.

The dialectic that by nature exists everywhere is denied by culturally imposed structures, but these very structures are self-destroying. In the impulse to be "I," the central point of the universe in whose shadow every other "sun" is buried or eclipsed (to use another of the novel's images) an individual assumes a permanent place of privilege that, in fact, proves disastrous, since he or she truly exists only in the "eye" of the other. Recontextualized in the realm of aesthetics, the principle is that the novel that privileges one I/eye--one point of view--is an oppressive, self-destroying structure that consolidates a system of assumed values and attempts to persuade the reader. In *Genesis*, the "I-narrator" as literary convention is used self-consciously, drawing attention to the concept of an authoritative and privileged point of view. Harris's final parodic twist is the concluding signature, "F.W.," coming at the end of the letter Wellington is reading. The signature announces that Wellington's co-respondent is, in fact "F.W." himself; writer and reader are one: active "I" and reflective "eye." Thus as writer and reader enter into "correspondence," the absolute authority of authorship is lost. Dialogue takes its place, and the reader outside the text may become the writer, the creator. Harris overturns another literary convention in introducing diagrammatic representations on the pages of his text. If, on the one hand, there is a dissolving of the boundaries between actual and fictive, between historical record and remembered anecdote, there is, on the other, a refusal to polarize art and science. The surveyor in the artist and the artist in the surveyor becomes a paradigm for the dialogic response to reality.

Point of view, then, and the limited perspective of the I/eye are major concerns of Harris in this novel, and one of the ways he approaches this concern technically is through characterization. Each character, or "agent,"[30] to use Harris's preferred term, has a restricted vision, the limitations of which are challenged or corrected by another, antithetical viewpoint. Frank Wellington, modern technological man, meets his opposite, for instance, in Reddy, the Amerindian instrument carrier. Reddy's simple faith that it is the "father of mountains" who "measures all creatures with the pole of the sun" (p. 121), is a measure of the limitations of Western expiricism, assuming in godlike stance that everything can be contained in a language of material measure-ment--theodolite and dumpy level. Similarly, Reddy's mystic interpretation of reality is challenged by the scientific data Wellington sets before him.

A similar pattern emerges in the pairing of two other crew members, Cummings Day and Moseley Adams. As if in denial of his given name, Cummings Day makes no optimistic sallies into the future, and studiously avoids the "heresy of expectations" (p. 89). Yet his counterpart, Moseley Adams, despite the patriarchal solidity of his name, is a revolutionary. Substituting for Day's "portrait of extinctions" his own "hammer of expectations" he is eager for change: "Is the devil's organization working people need, not communist god. To organize is to arm. I want to take a course in aerodynamics, Skipper. I want to learn about propellers, aeroplanes. I want to sit in a chair and sail and fly" (p. 90). Implicitly, through the opposition of "portrait" and "hammer" the text invites consideration of the relationship between art and politics or between art and technology in any process that will influence the "coming day" for "Adams" of the New World.

Yet another reciprocal pairing is that of Ada and Marti Fredericks. Ada is a sturdy peasant woman whose exterior betrays little of the richness within. It takes the revised reading that Wellington now engages in to see, within her gesture of offering bread and fish to her man, a revelation of a fertility goddess filling the land. Conversely, wealthy capitalist Marti Fredericks, head of an Indian family who own a countrywide chain of stores and boarding houses, is ironically seen as "a mere stick of a man on which to hang a flag" (p. 103). Where he appears to own everything in sight, he is, in fact, impoverished. His history-making conquests are a mere row of flags, standing "in ironic contrast to Ada's overpowering apron, landscape" (p.103).

The male bonding evident in the economic enterprises of the Fredericks brothers leads to oppressive exploitation of the surrounding folk and landscape, and to a hollow deprivation at the core of their own "house"--"their fasting blood, their fasting bone" (p. 104). Harris takes their story and works it into a myth, his stated aim in *Genesis* being "to create an imaginative equation for anecdotes of incest . . . to embody [incest] with a dimension of profound significance so that it can acquire something akin to the purification of tragedy."[31]   And indeed the story of the Fredericks brothers' initiation into an incestuous capitalist tribe is a twentieth-century rewrite of Freud's version of the Oedipus myth.

Freud hypothesizes that the notion of incest is the basis of all social structure.[32]   The universal human taboo on incest, he suggests, stems from an aboriginal situation in which the tribal father possesses all the women. The sons, in order to appropriate the womenfolk and assert their manhood, slay the father, but are subsequently overcome with guilt. Out of their guilt come the various kinship observances in human society.   Harris takes the concept that a system of tyranny grew out of a situation of scarcity and applies it to many aspects of Guyanese society--sexual, economic, and political.   Society's tribal impulses are thus discovered to be based on illusory fears. Tyranny consists of reinforcing the fears and guarding tribal boundaries still more frenetically; freedom is gained by confronting the perhaps illusory fears on which tyranny builds.   The crucial point, though, revealed in Hope's discourse on the ratio of women to men is that present scarcity is a fiction.

Fictive or no, scarcity and deprivation, the novel asserts, are the basis of Western ideology. Capitalism preconceives wealth not as a relationship, but as an entity, thus creating a void, an absence that is poverty; history is the written text, while the unrecorded is a silent emptiness; progress is defined in quantifiable, material terms, so that the life of the spirit is absent. Symbolic of this ideology premised upon the void of deprivation and scarcity is the marketplace in *Genesis of the Clowns*, where money assumes a godlike stance.   Here, even the landscape reflects the mercenary quest for gold that first drove men to seek a new world: "There were evenings when the sun rolled down the sky and vanished all of a sudden like a huge coin within the till of the savannas" (pp. 107-108).

The marketplace itself is an expression of the mercantilist spirit that has imposed its order on the land. Everything is for sale there. Behind the fish and vegetables, behind the clock and theodolite, behind the neatly dressed figure of Miss Ada at her stall, lurks a surrealistic vision of man's labor, his creativity, his intelligence, his body, his time and the very land he walks upon being put up for sale. As the narrator looks toward the "coming day," he sees no life springing from such barren investment: "Cummings Day stood at the edge of sunset, economic target of the past and the future when all expectations subsided, drained away into nothingness. The till of the globe rang up the changes, rang up buttoned-up hopes, pursed lips, featureless wealth" (p.108). Brutal reification of humanity and the destruction of the essential oneness of life by its division into saleable portions is surrealistically portrayed as a butcher's shop in which a "blind man" points to "a stall with foetal divisions of meat reflected in a sunset world" (p. 111). The "tyranny of the emotions" built into contemporary Guyanese society--political and economic exploitation--has its beginning, then, in Europe's quest for El Dorado, her materialistic orientation, her mercantilist drive. The Fredericks brothers operate a love-hate economy that jealously keeps wealth within the tribe, exploiting those outside. Hope's worldview, shaped by slavery, has no picture for noneconomic relations. "I always believe a man is chained to his deeds. We buy one another, we sell one another in chains" (p. 141), he confesses. As shaman, though, the author seeks a spiritual genesis, a return to origins that will renew, re-create his world. He seeks a world in which the gold of El Dorado is perceived not as material acquisition but as spiritual riches.

Under capitalist ideology, everything is rendered saleable--land and time, labor and song. But in the very situation where humanity is thus reified, where human flesh is put on sale, the trickster-god of the marketplace resides. Money walks godlike "on stilts," and Frank Wellington's skills fetch a "good price, a god's price" in the market. Nevertheless, concealed within the measuring tools of material domination and cupidity--the "cupid" clock and the surveyor's theodolite dividing time and space into marketable portions--a countermovement appears in the figure of Anancy and his web: "Cupids stood hand in hand with anancy figures inscribed on a battered clock. The theodolite had intrigued me. It possessed an old-fashioned telescope within which the markings on the diaphragm used to be made with spider's web" (p. 96).

The godlike stilts on which money walks in the market are seen also where Chung lives in his lonely outpost in the interior. Chung in his "stilted" watchtower, dipping imagined future gold by the bucketful out of the river, is complemented by Hope in his cavelike Albouystown slum dwelling. Chung strains eagerly into a rich future made possible by technological harnessing of natural resources; Hope reaches back to a rich but buried heritage symbolized in the Albouystown Old Glory African Masquerade Band. In these two figures, Harris explores the "limbo-anancy syndrome" outlined earlier in this chapter. For Chung and Hope, living in hinterland and ghetto, are liminal figures, materially deprived but possessing spiritual wealth.

   Both Chung and Hope are mask wearers, masqueraders. Victor Turner discusses the use of symbolic animal masks in liminal rituals. He suggests they communicate an antistructural mode by replacing culture with nature:

> Thus it is in liminality and also in those phases of ritual that abut on liminality that one finds profuse symbolic reference to beasts, birds, and vegetation. Animal masks, bird plumage, grass fibres, garments of leaves swathe and enshroud the human neophytes and priests. Thus, symbolically, their structural life is snuffed out by animality and nature, even as it is being regenerated by these very same forces. One dies *into* nature to be reborn *from* it.[33]

Chung, in his retreat from society, is to find in nature resources for a powerful renewal of society. Shamanlike, he wears an animal mask; indeed, he is so transformed that he seems part of the leafy world around him: "Chung's brow and face looked parchment-dry like a leaf drained of all moisture . . . . His ears were uplifted into an animal's mask penetrated by a twig, a branch, every sound, every sign, in rain-forest or river" (p. 130). The vision afforded him moves far beyond the structure of records and statistics used by the surveying team to make predictions about the future. He believes simply "that the river will rise one day like a bucket of gold" (p. 133). Formal record and rationalized deduction are irrelevant to the inner vision that sustains him. Gradually the narrator sees the vision, too:

> For here . . . an alchemisation of comedy of divinity had begun to happen, however secretly, that would serve to invest an absurd watch-tower at the heart of the bush with a cornerstone of gold. Serve to invest it with the stilted outlines of the future implicit to flood and drought--the coming of electricity, the ghostly crowds that would swarm, the gold rush, the playing fields, the distant roar of traffic from the waterfalls, the skeleton hand on an upturned bucket at the side of the river on which Hope banged, a steel drum, an orchestra, a carnival. (p. 134)

From his liminal position, communicated through images of

death (malaise of the bush), alchemy (fire and gold), and of oneness with nature, Chung is able to see beyond his present material deprivation to a rich future. Hope, in contrast, lives crouched in his "cave," in the shadow of the past. Like Chung, Hope and the masqueraders of Albouystown step out of structure into a carnival world of "natural" beauty. Shedding his "tattered trousers and vest" (p. 138), Hope will appear in one of Lucille's rich costumes--"dresses and shirts and shawls into which had been threaded life-like brilliant designs like futuristic stamps, butterflies, sunflowers, blood-red cherries, starapples" (p. 139). As the narrator looks at Hope's face, the light seems to give it "a masked, a dead appearance" (p. 140). Implicit in this momentary revelation is the question of whether it is Hope's finery or his tattered poverty that constitutes the mask--or whether neither "mask" truly reveals Hope, himself.

Chung in his stilted, futuristic pose and Hope in his cave, retreating into the past, are the twin figures of the limbo dance. Together they inhabit a limbo present, straddled between dreams. Each of them, too, embodies a "collision of culture" that contains, in Harris's view, the seed for renewal. Chung's dream draws together natural resources and technological skill; Hope's memory evokes past glory of both African and European-- cultural heritage--ancestral masks on the one hand, Christmas and the estate house on the other. Together, the dancer on the ground and the dancer on stilts parody the godlike and the humbled--implying that *both* positions are merely moments in a dance.

The dance, then, is a symbolic reassembling of the dismem-bered god--a celebration of survival. In it there is a creative accommodation to the change in fortune. Albouystown and La Penitence, now the site of disagreeable tenements, were once, the narrator tells us, the site of an eighteenth-century estate owned by a religious French landowner. And the past still lives, in fragments, in the architecture of the area: "In the midst of the present dilapidation there suddenly appeared what was unmis-takably a motif of the past, something that reminded one of a high window that may have dominated the estate, a tressised figure or relic of centrality relating to ruling architectural premises, a clue to a code of manners or appearances that once ruled the labouring flat earth on every hand" (p. 136-137).

The area and its residents share a depressed character, yet even here in the depths of deprivation and poverty there is, in the narrator's vision, a countermovement. As the tenements fall down around them, the stilt dancers rise up. Within the "weather-- beaten, unpainted slum of an old three-storey house" (p. 138), the costumes Lucille has stitched--another image of fragments creatively drawn together--breathe a spirit of life into the room, turning the gloomy cave into a "womb of light" and tattered clowns into dancing gods.

Besides the old French plantation house in whose ruins Hope now lives, another historical building looms on the landscape--the ruins of the Dutch fort, Kyk-over-al. The narrator ponders on the building of the fort and its possible state in the future when it might be site for "a city museum . . . with bridges spanning the waters on either hand" (p. 125). Punning on muse/museum, Harris converts the fort into a museum--a place where the past is framed into art, fragments rearranged and recontextualized in such a way that they invite reflective contemplation. History used creatively in this manner loses its threatening authority and becomes a means of growth, as one draws meaning from the apparent fragmentation and disorder of reality. Only thus will mankind be inspired to build bridges (communication) and cities (relationships) instead of fortified castles. Kyk-over-al turned "museum" becomes, then, another dimension of the reassembly of a dismembered god.[34]

Harris's own novel reflects the new configuration or relationship implied in this image. Historical event is removed from the world of action and made an artifact among other framed memories, which reflect upon each other to provide a myth--a source of wisdom in place of a dominating structure of oppression.[35] Once again the point is made that the novel in the New World must avoid formal structures that (like history) impose an arbitrary, persuasive view. Rather, a museumlike arrangement or juxtaposition of objects is required, among which the reader, outside of the familiar time-span ordering of sequential reality, *muses* freely, making his own connections and inferences. Such an art of the grotesque declares that creativity is not the privilege solely of the artist; each reader of reality, of the "text," is invited to re-create the world for himself.

Harris's love of literary intertextuality thus makes the point that each new beholder of reality gathers together its fragments to shape a unique vision. The notion of "authority," both in the sense of a uniquely gifted individual and in that of canonized texts, is thus implicitly rejected: the "House" of literary tradition crumbles before the Anancy-artist, who insists that at every moment creation begins anew, that possibilities for new configurations are infinite. The threatening gun/cannon/ canon is only a phallus after all, "dying" in the womb of each new mind before it can bring forth new life.

The narrator's musing on the crumbling grandeur of European structure is thus a metaphoric comment on the structure of the novel and a discussion of authorship as authoritarian assumption. His problem is how to convert the novel, "a haunted shell in which a jealous . . . estate landowner shot his wife" (p. 145), into a womb of life in which dialogue with the reader, a kind of fruitful "intercourse," supersedes the authoritarian mode of persuasion:

I wondered indeed as I looked around whether the devaluation of premises I now saw on every hand had actually lain concealed from the very beginning within a formal beautiful facade as the absurd gift of life to life susceptible to seemliness or unseemliness according to one's tragic or involved or insensible point of view. And if so what therapy of re-imagination, re-evaluation of the mystery of love, the mystery of freedom one possessed for the epidemic disease of wealth one saw unconcealed on every hand in the ash and tattered flare of ancient masters and modern slaves, ancient mistresses and modern clowns. (p. 138)

The very name Albouystown brings us full circle to where we started with the flag-bearing buoys in the Abary River. Just as the buoys in the Abary indicated a depth movement counter to the surface flow, so the folk of Albouystown stand in mythic relationship to the tide of history that flows from the old glory of European and African past to a present state of decay. Out of the buoyancy of the folk there is hope of a newly created world-- cave becomes womb.

Such a paradox of revolutionary and counterrevolutionary forces appears, too, in the prevailing imagery of *Genesis*. The story line or "history" of the novel has a clustering of vocabulary suggesting action, measurement, and energy harnessed by man for both constructive and destructive purposes: "strike," "hammer," "rivet," "blow," "bullet," "gun," "theodolite." These images of material progress are counterbalanced by a different force, paradoxically frail yet vigorous: "pollen," "seed," "breath," "space," "dance," "landscape." Between the structures of dominance and control breathes a spirit of life and renewal--Anancy spinning in the Great House.

Similarly, the conventional forward-moving narrative thread encounters a contrary flow in the reflective point of view, which reassembles the past other than chronologically. Abundant use of puns discredits authoritarian statement and evokes the "telling silences secreted in the family of the Word" (p. 148). Anecdote and letter, rumor and nonverbal signifying take their place over against the recorded text and the spoken word, so that in focusing on the insignificant doodles at history's margins, Harris expresses the belief that "nothing can be deemed insignificant or accidental in the product of the human spirit."[36]

Finally, we turn to consideration of the narrator himself. Wellington's experience--an experience duplicated as one reads the novel--is a rite of passage. Repeatedly, Wellington is required to abandon former "devalued" premises, and deconstruct his "text" of the past, dying into new awareness as the "ridge pole" of material construction falls on him. For Frank Wellington, like

the reader, is gazing not into an objective reality, but into a
mirror in which he sees himself. Each of the men in the team is
a "reflection" of Wellington. Hope wears "Wellington boots,"
Moseley Adams, like Wellington, is an airplane pilot *manque*, and
the mercenary orientation of the Persauds reflects Wellington
seated at his "paytable." When we discover that Hope has indeed
shot (black) Frank Wellington, that Wellington's correspondent is
"F.W.," and that Hope (who is first seen pointing a gun at
Wellington) has killed himself, we realize that all the men are
natives of Wellington's person, all "agents" in whom he discovers
the limitations of his "I"--his point of view.[37]

There is a further curiosity about the signature, "F.W."
Conventionally, a signature expresses authorship, authority; but
in this instance ambivalence is introduced since the signature is
shared by Frank Wellington and his correspondent. Their
reading/writing of reality is a shared experience, a dialogue.
Derrida's wordplay regarding the iterability of the word--its
difference/differance--comes to mind.[38] His argument is that
not only do words have different meanings in different contexts,
but that there is a certain deferring of meaning so that each
reflection on the utterance reveals new dimensions of signification. Harris's use of the signature thus assumes and denies
privileged authorship. It implies, in fact, the "absence" of the
signatory,[39] declaring that each new reading is a recontextualiza-
tion, a reconfiguration of reality: "each present illumination
shifts the debris of the past a little" (p. 82).

In effect, then, Harris takes his thesis that "light" exists
between, not within, given constructs, and applies it to the
individual person. Frank Wellington wears different masks at
different times: he is the White surveyor with a fine shock of
hair keeping a polite distance from Lucille in Guyana, but he is
also her bald, dark-skinned lover at the Trinidad Carnival. Each
person has his "carnival" side--the paradoxical counterpart to the
everyday public mask. Recognition of such a "comedy of opposite
investitures" (p. 147) of the reality within and outside of one's
person, Frank Wellington learns, is a step toward the humility
and compassion that save from totalitarian attitudes and their
tragic consequences. Carnival's burlesque mask wearing is a
healthy reminder of the falsity and partial nature of the "faces"
humanity assumes. The essential human spirit dwells in paradox.

Europe's assumed authority and sovereignty made the West
Indian into a mere shadow--a clown--and her history denied him
any place as hero in the drama. The same process is repeated in
any totalitarian assumption of power that silences opposition and
refuses dialogue. Nevertheless, in the inversions of carnival, the
fool assumes kingly office, revealing by his burlesque performance the inadequacy of humanity to take up authoritarian
positions. Enid Welsford describes the type of society in which

the fool's burlesque will flourish, and her description is a significant comment, in the context of this present discussion, on the assumed sanctity of European overlordship: "The King, the Priest, and the Fool all belong to the same regime, all belong essentially to a society shaped by belief in Divine order, human inadequacy, efficacious ritual . . . . The fool in cap and bells can only flourish among people who have sacraments, who value symbols as well as tools, and cannot forever survive the decay of faith if in divinely imposed authority, the rejection of all taboo and mysterious inspiration."[40]

Enid Welsford draws an important distinction between hero and fool. The "serious hero," she says, "focuses events, forces issues, and causes catastrophes; but the Fool by his mere presence dissolves events, evades issues, and throws doubt on the finality of fact."[41]

Evasiveness, doubt, and paradox are the elements in which both Fool and his counterpart, Trickster, dwell. And Harris's technique partakes of this carnival atmosphere. Art, in his hands, thus becomes a necessary check on dominant social assumptions. As the clown is to the king, so the Anancy-spirit of the folk (artist) is to the House of authoritarian premise. Mr Hate-to-be--Contradicted desperately needs to see the void at the core of his stately edifice of certainties, the darkness within his sun's "eye."

The polarizations of oppressive structure create a tragic world. Between structured opposites, though, is the "light" of a comic vision--a vision of equality, of communitas, of laughter. Trickster's denial of structure's assumptions, his evasion of the role of sacrificial scapegoat, his stress on the paradox of life are the fertile gateways to a New World "comedy of light."

NOTES

1. Literature on the trickster includes Barbara Babcock-Abrahams, "'A Tolerated Margin of Mess': The Trickster and His Tales Reconsidered," *Journal of the Folklore Institute* 11 (1975), 147-186; Norman O. Brown, *Hermes the Thief: The Evolution of a Myth* (New York: Random House, 1969); Laura Makarius, "Ritual Clowns and Symbolic Behavior," *Diogenes* 69 (1970): 44-73; Robert D. Pelton, *The Trickster in West Africa: A Study of Mythic Irony and Sacred Delight* (Berkeley: University of California Press, 1980); Paul Radin, *The Trickster: A Study in American Indian Mythology* (New York: Greenwood Press, 1956); Barre Toelke, "The 'Pretty Language' of Yellowman: Genre, Mode and Texture in Navaho Coyote Narratives," Genre 2: 3 (1969); Victor W. Turner, "Myth and Symbol," in *International Encyclopedia of the Social Sciences* (New York: Macmillan, 1968); and Joan Wescott, "The Sculpture and Myths of Eshu-Elegba, the

Yoruba Trickster," *Africa* 32 (1962).

2. Babcock-Abrahams, "Margin," p. 186.

3. Pelton, *Trickster*, p. 224.

4. Babcock-Abrahams,"Margin," p. 154.

5. Pelton, *Trickster*, p. 37.

6. Ibid., p. 60.

7. The following information on spiders is taken from *Dictionnaire des Symboles* (Paris: Seghers, 1969).

8. Makarius, "Clowns," p. 46.

9. Ibid., p. 54.

10. Harvey Cox, *The Feast of Fools* (Cambridge, Mass.: Harvard University Press, 1969), p. 141.

11. Ibid., p. 134.

12. Ibid., p. 145.

13. Makarius, "Clowns," p. 61.

14. Henry Louis Gates, Jr., "The 'Blackness of Blackness': A Critique of the Sign and the Signifying Monkey," *Critical Inquiry* 9 (June 1983), p. 686.

15. Ibid., p. 688.

16. Jack Derrida, "Structure, Sign, and Play in the Discourse of the Human Sciences," in *Of Grammatology*, trans. Gayatri Spivak (Baltimore: Johns Hopkins University Press, 1976). Derrida acknowledges his indebtedness to Levi-Strauss, who introduces the notion of the social scientist as *bricoleur*, engaged in a mythopoetical activity.

17. Ian Munro and Reinhard Sander, eds., *Kas-Kas: Interviews with Three Caribbean Writers in Texas* (Austin: University of Texas Press, 1972), p. 13.

18. Wakdjunkaga, trickster of the Winnebago Indians, possesses both characteristics--weaving skill and enormous phallus.

19. Munro and Sander, *Kas-Kas*, p. 45.

20. Derek Walcott, "Juvenilia." (Housed at the University of the West Indies.)

21. Wa Thiong'o Ngugi, *Homecoming: Essays on African and Caribbean Literature, Culture, and Politics* (London: Heinemann Educational Books, 1972), p. 125.

22. Jean Piaget, *The Child and Reality* (New York: Grossman Publishers, 1973), p. 10.

23. Ibid., p. 16. In *Genesis of the Clowns*, Wilson Harris describes as a Copernican revolution the shift in perception that occurs when individuals and cultures become "aware of themselves as satellite never sovereign," (p. 117).

24. Clifford Geertz, "Deep Play: Notes on the Balinese Cockfight," *Interpretation of Cultures*, pp. 412-453. In examining the elaborate system of conventions observed in cockfights among the Balinese people, Clifford Geertz comes to the conclusion that the cockfight provides metasocial commentary and that its function is interpretative: "it is a Balinese reading of Balinese

experience, a story they tell themselves about themselves." It is interesting to note, too, in connection with Gordon's story, that trickster's genitals may act independently. In Radin's account, mischief is done by Wakdjunkaga's ambulatory genitals, while the trickster himself remains at home.

25. Edward Kamau Brathwaite, "All God's Chillun," in *Rights of Passage* (London: Oxford University Press, 1967), p. 18.

26. John Thieme, "The Legacy of Conquest--An Interview with Wilson Harris" *Caribbean Contact*, March 1980, p. 17. Quotations that follow are all from this article.

27. Wilson Harris, "History, Fable, and Myth in the Caribbean and the Guianas," in *Anagogic Qualities of literature*, ed. Joseph P. Strelka (University Park and London: Pennsylvania State University Press, 1971), pp. 120-131. Citations that follow are all from this article.

28. Wilson Harris, "Interior of the Novel: Amerindian/European/African Relations," in *National Identity: Papers Delivered at the Commonwealth Literature Conference, University of Queensland* (Brisbane, August 9-15, 1968), ed. K. L. Goodwin (London: Heinemann Press, 1970), p. 138.

29. Martin Heidegger, *Poetry, Language, and Thought*, trans. Albert Hofstadter (New York: Harper, 1971), p. 182.

30. "Within the new art of fiction we are attempting to explore, ... it is a 'vacancy' in nature within which agents appear who are translated one by the other and who (in a kind of serial illumination--if 'serial' is the right word) reappear through each other, inhabit each other, reflect a burden of necessity, push each other to plunge into the unknown, into the translatable, transmutable legacies of history." Harris, "Interior of the Novel," p. 146.

31. Wilson Harris, "Aspects of the Exploration of History," unpublished lecture, University of Guyana, March 15, 1978.

32. Sigmund Freud, *Totem and Taboo*, trans. J. Strachey (New York: Norton, 1952).

33. Victor Turner, *Dramas, Fields, and Metaphors* (Ithaca, N.Y.: Cornell University Press, 1974), p. 253.

34. This reading, in which the artist in his mythmaking supersedes the historian in his presumed reconstruction of material data, is further strengthened when we recall that Kyk-over-al was the name chosen for the literary journal, edited by Arthur J. Seymour, in which a number of Harris's early poems and essays appeared.

35. Harris's response to history is not unlike that of Friedrich Nietzsche as expressed in his 1873 essay, "The Use and Abuse of History," trans. Adrian Collins (New York: Liberal Arts Press, 1957).

36. Anton Ehrenzweig, *The Hidden Order of Art* (Berkeley: University of California Press, 1969), p. 27.

37. "This 'I' which approaches the text is already itself a plurality of other texts, of codes which are infinite or, more precisely, lost (whose origins are lost)." Roland Barthes, *S/Z* (New York: Hill and Wang, 1974), p. 10.

38. Jacques Derrida, "Difference," in *Speech and Phenomena*, trans. David B. Allison (Evanston: Northwestern University Press, 1973), pp. 129-160.

39. Jacques Derrida, "Signature, Event, Context," *Glyph 3* 1 (Baltimore: Johns Hopkins University Press, 1976), pp. 172-197.

40. Enid Welsford, *The Fool: His Social and Literary History* (Gloucester, Mass.: Faber and Faber, 1966), p. 195.

41. Ibid., p. xii.

III

The Controlling I-Eye

The Arawak woman pointed and Vigilance, straining his mind from the volcanic precipice where he clung, looked and saw the blue ring of pentecostal fire in God's eye as it wheeled around him above the dreaming memory and prison of life until it melted where neither wound nor witch stood. (Wilson Harris, *Palace of the Peacock*)

To this point my discussion has tended to focus chiefly on male characters: on Chiki and G, on Cristo and the surveying team led by Frank Wellington. The quotation cited above from Harris's *Palace of the Peacock*, however, surely invites a feminist perspective and a shift in critical vocabulary. Here a folk figure, a woman, is the principal "signifier" as she points, directing the laboring Vigilance toward his own moment of vision. Through the Arawak woman's tutelage, Vigilance sees no longer a sacrificial cross (wound and witch) of structured premises, but a "god's eye" of wholeness. Circularity suggested in "ring" and "wheeled" presents a feminine image of wholeness that invites Vigilance to abandon the threatening "volcanic precipice" and containing "prison" of his premises.

In this chapter, I propose to employ a feminist perspective in approaching Harris's *Palace of the Peacock* and Lamming's *Natives of My Person*. Both novels are patterned on early voyages of exploration and plunder in the New World, and both have an all-male crew as their chief protagonists. Yet both novels give prominent place to a silent yet signifying feminine Other, an autochthonous power linked with the land that offers both a promise of virgin delights and a threat of destruction. The women in both novels are denied a place in the historical action.

All (except Mariella whose name is that of the mission she inhabits) are nameless, without identity. The men, in contrast, thrust aggressively into the New World, and have, if not names, at least identities created by their various professional statuses. (Just how authentic these names and identities are remains to be seen). One might say, in a word, that the men have assumed the role of "I" while the women are observers of action, "eyes" reflecting acts and images of husbands, lovers--and rapists.

The very visual form of the written characters "I"-"eye" links the "I" with the masculine and the "eye" with the feminine. The solitary "I"--erect, phallic, and aggressive--invites a verb, names action and intention. The "eye"--womblike, embracing--is more feminine. It implies the seer, the see-er, and the seen; reflection and imagination.

The discussion that follows will examine the role of the "I-eye" in *Palace* and *Natives*, attempting to uncover the writer's position on ontological and existential questions that must be answered by those who live in a landscape dominated by another's House. Principles of inclusion and exclusion, arbitrary decisions to prefer or reject, such as the house model betrays, are simply a matter of point of view. These principles and decisions are, ultimately, creations of an I-eye dichotomy. Any single I-eye perceives from its own peculiar position. An I-eye facing it will see quite differently. One problem with Houses, though, is that their very permanence implicitly denies alternative worldviews: the "I" assumes total sovereignty, failing in this assumption to become an "eye," "womb of light" as it were, in which the other can be imaged and birthed. The person seen by the "I" is forever objectified, reified.

Both novels lay bare this hostile polarization of the "I" and the "eye," where, ideally, there ought to be a dynamic relationship or marriage. The epic thrust of man's history making will be seen (to use Harris's metaphor) as a prolonged "erection" of the I into a rocklike phallic edifice that has failed to impregnate the womb of nature. Only when that I "dies" in the womb of a reflective eye will humankind be reborn. When the colonized Other of the world--its poor, its underprivileged, its women, indeed all the outcasts of Western patriarchal economies, are released from bondage and the earth itself is caressed and honored instead of plundered and raped, only then will a truly New World be birthed.

Colonization of the Other, the naming of that Other as monstrous Caliban (cannibal), is an economic transaction, an "economy," in which the self purchases its identity with currency generated by the devaluation of the Other. Recognition and honoring of the Other begin within the self as a decolonization of repressed elements of the psyche. Such repressed impulses that are projected onto a monstrous Other must, as Harris puts it, be recognized as being "native to psyche," and brought back into the self. Only by this means will thought be liberated from the "implacable polarizations" that hinder the creative spirit. Harris's argument is that the meeting point of the polarized worlds within the person (and likewise the meeting point where cultures collide in heterogeneous societies) is potentially the ground of creativity. French feminist writer Helene Cixous makes a similar point, stressing the creative potential of the Other within the I--the "homosexual component." This androgynous character, which she names "homosexuality," alone makes creativity possible:

> But there is no *invention* possible, whether it be philosophical or poetic, without the presence in the investigating subject of an abundance of the other, of the diverse: persons detached, persons thought, peoples born of the unconscious, and in each desert, suddenly animated, a springing forth of self that we did not know about--our women, our monsters, our jackals, our Arabs, our fellow creatures, our fears. But there is no invention of other I's, no poetry, no fiction without a certain homosexuality (interplay therefore of bisexuality) making in me a crystallized work of my ultrasubjectivities.[1]

Cixous's feminist perspective is introduced here because in both the novels to be discussed in this chapter, the colonizer is associated through the imagery with the masculine, and the colonized with the feminine. In the vision of Helene Cixous, the alterity of the masculine within the feminine and the feminine within the masculine is recognized as the source of creative potential. But in the polarized world criticized by Lamming and Harris, the feminine has been colonized by the masculine: the womb transformed into a tomb. The two novelists depict a hierarchized system that can only be destructive.

Colonization is effectively achieved through language, Lamming argues (following Fanon). Feminist writers echo this in their assault on the "logocentrism" and assumed author-ity of the wielder of the pen (penis). For Lamming, the experience of being colonized is, in fact, primarily a confinement within the linguistic structures of the colonizer. In his discussion of *The Tempest*, he explores the meaning for Caliban of confinement to expression in Prospero's language. He explains, "Prospero has given Caliban language, and with it an unstated history of consequences, an unknown history of future intentions. This gift of language meant not English, in particular, but speech and concept as a way, a method, a necessary avenue towards areas of the self which could not be reached in any other way . . . . Language is the very prison in which Caliban's achievements will be released and restricted."[2]

Language, of course, is essentially metaphorical. It is Prospero who has created the notion of *virgin* lands, of a new world, of his own role as the *prosperous* one whose mission is to subject and control through the "magic" of his science and technology, planting his flag of sovereignty. It is Prospero who *names* Caliban, Prospero who introduces the notion of the mother-witch, thus projecting on the nature around him his own nightmare fantasy that the pastoral retreat might prove to be not a virgin's womb and embrace, but a devouring maw--the "vagina dentata" of brute nature that must be dominated with whips and scourges. And as he "names" the land, so it is--for him.

A number of women writers, in examining the controlling metaphors in male texts, have pointed to the way in which their authors have projected their own psychological conflicts onto the reality they attempt to represent. Further, such metaphors have become the reality. Behavior has been determined by the fictive metaphors rather than by intrinsic demands of nature itself. Man's arbitrary naming of the world reveals his own inner turbulence "writ large" on nature, which takes on the image of a polarized psyche.

Literary critic Annette Kolodny exposes such habits of naming in the writing of male American authors from the earliest settlers in the New World to the present. Her Freudian psychohistory of male American texts reveals an ambivalence in attitudes toward the land, an ambivalence that she locates in the root metaphor identifying the land as woman. Unable to determine whether the land is a sweetheart virgin or a mother figure, male writers waver between a desire to conquer and master on the one hand and filial submissiveness on the other. Kolodny reads between the lines of texts written on the American landscape a thinly veiled expression of conflicting masculine drives: the drive for individuation expressed in sexual aggressiveness and the drive for nurturing through union with the maternal. The mother/virgin image of the land is problematic, she explains, because within the terms of the controlling metaphor, masculine interaction with the landscape becomes either a rape or an incestuous union. Passivity is no solution either, for nature, unaided, will not satisfy man's needs: "If activity inevitably confers the guilt of violation--and, even more threatening, the guilt of an incestuous violation--the desire to experience the natural world passively is similarly self-defeating. For all her promise, her bounty, her seductive beauty, nature must finally be made to provide for man; he dare not wait for all to be given [for] salvation comes through activity not passivity."[3] Repeatedly frustrated by the refusal of a landscape he has named Mother and Mistress to bountifully satisfy his desires, man responds in angry frustration and attempts ruthlessly to dominate the land. His technological achievements have increasingly made this possible until what began as a romance with a virgin land and a reclining on a maternal bosom become the "single-minded destruction and pollution of the continent."[4]

For the early settlers in the "virgin lands" of the New World, the uncontrollable element in nature was the native male-Caliban. This rival for nature's favors in lands possessed by right of conquest became at once a negative image of the invaders' lust. Mutual fears of cannibalism and rape of the womenfolk, of castration and of abnormal sexual appetite in the other racial group are all predominantly male preoccupations arising, quite probably, from the premise that names the lands "virgin." All of these fears emerge more or less overtly in the two West Indian novels of conquest I shall discuss.

Kolodny's argument is that Western society has become trapped by the metaphor in which it originally sought to contain nature and that the initial premise of that metaphor is man's imaging of nature as feminine. Employing a feminist perspective in her study of the scientific revolution of the sixteenth and seventeenth centuries, Carolyn Merchant makes discoveries similar to Kolodny's. Merchant's study traces the changing metaphors that accompanied the growth of scientific knowledge and technological expertise in the period she analyzes. The organic view of the cosmos that upheld the image of nature as nurturing mother was gradually to give place to the image of nature as witch, as a dangerous mystery to be probed and analyzed so that man's God-given dominion over the earth--dominion he lost in the Fall--might be regained, and the curse of the Fall reversed. She shows how historical witch burnings and improved technology for harnessing the forces of nature for man's benefit stand side by side with texts rich in metaphors of torture and inquisition. Thus man by his metaphors justifies his violent restraint of and probing into the mysteries of the Other, which is always feminine.

Pre-Copernican cosmology, then, which presented the sun as satellite to the female earth, coincided with the image of earth as a virgin to be wooed by her courtly lover. The Copernican revolution, though, took the throne from the female earth and gave it to the masculine sun. The earth must now keep to her allotted orbit lest the whole course of nature be disrupted. Restraint of the wayward feminine became necessary for the sake of social stability. Metaphor thus emerges as a political tool; as Carolyn Merchant says, "The interrogation of witches as symbol for the interrogation of nature, the courtroom as model for its inquisition, and torture through mechanical devices as a tool for the subjugation of disorder were fundamental to the scientific method as power."[5]

The final major step that Merchant identifies is the shift to an image of the cosmos as inorganic clockwork--a mechanistic notion that has permeated Western consciousness to the present. While nature was a woman, delving and mining into the pits and holes of her "body" involved sexual overtones that betrayed the insatiable lust of man. Nature imaged as a mechanical device, however, offered no such problem. As soon an he had pronounced the death of nature in metaphor, man could proceed to effect her destruction in reality. Commercial capitalism could now proceed unfettered.   Both Kolodny and Merchant conclude with the same observation: there is need to step outside the metaphors that control a worldview if a new relationship between man and nature is to be created. Writers in our own age, Kolodny notes, have attempted to get away from the "notion of the land as something to be either exclusively possessed or preyed upon--like a sexual object--and suggest instead, an intimacy based on reciprocity and communality."[6] The ability to step outside our metaphors may endeed be the way to salvation. As Kolodny says, "Such may, in fact, be man's ultimate creative act: to pick and choose among the image systems available to him at any one time and to make of them, periodically, a new reality. Perhaps, to put it another way, we need to 'wake up' to our ability to dream the as-yet-unknown and unconventional."[7] Merchant's conclusion echoes Kolodny's, adding the caution that, since metaphors are political investments, recovery of a sense of the essential dynamism of the cosmos and the interrelatedness of all its organs will be effected "only by a reversal of mainstream values and a revolution in economic priorities."[8] Restated in the terms of our present discussion, this is to say that the "eye," reflecting and giving birth to image, may be a means of salvation for the aggressive, history-making "I" that seems bent on destruction both of itself and of the womb that offers a hope for rebirth.

I propose, then, to draw together, within a feminist perspective, the twin problems of identity and language--of being "framed" by another's perception and "penned" in another's text. By shifting my focus to the feminine, I expect to discover a potential womb in which human hope and longings for fulfillment may yet be formed and brought into being. Such a strategy will reveal the complex psychological processes involved in the struggle for identity. It will lay bare, too, ideological and political investments that necessitate the continuing depreciation and exploitation of the Other. The web that I spin here, then, brings into relationship a number of themes in West Indian fiction: commerce, language, identity/community, folk heritage/-imposed culture, the nature of creativity, and, finally, the response of *homo ludens* to an increasingly oppressive, technology-controlled House.

In the two novels to be analyzed in this chapter, we return to the sixteenth and seventeenth centuries and the rape of virgin lands by European powers. Lamming's *Natives of My Person* is the story of a slave-trading vessel sailing the triangular route between Europe, the West Coast of Africa, and the colonies in the New World. Harris's plot line takes up the El Dorado legend and follows a small boatload of men as they journey up river into the Guyana hinterland in search of cheap labor for coastal estates. The two novels have much in common. They both create a myth from historical fact; both point to the destructiveness inherent in the polarizations established in the plantation economy that by no means ended with the abolition of slavery; and they both present the exploited land and folk in terms of the feminine. Finally, both novels make the point that polarized opposites must be drawn together again and the Other recognized as native to one's person if patterns of oppression and domination are to be obviated.

The landscape of Lamming's *Natives of My Person* describes a divided world in which the concept of imperialism is given mythic dimensions. The relationship of Great House to landscape emerges as a basic structure of human intercourse from which there appears to be no release. In every aspect of life, from the political and economic to the sexual, individuals and nations are bound to each other by oppressive ties in which they relate as victor to victim, oppressor to oppressed, exploiter to exploited. Further, at a psychological level, there exists within each individual a colony of repressed other selves--"natives" of the person--who threaten momently to overthrow that ego-bound impostor who seeks dominion.

The physical world of the novel sets the Kingdom of Lime Stone as the imperial power whose authority extends across the globe to the Isles of the Black Rock--San Cristobal. Rivaling the strength of Lime Stone is the power of Antarctica. The names of the players have changed, but the power struggle is easily recognized. From the days of Columbus and Hawkins, Raleigh and Cortez, to the present day rivalry of business kingdoms and superpowers, the game has been played according to much the same system of rules--the principles of economic self-interest, or, as Lamming puts it, according to the rules of "the House of Trade and Justice."

This body of authority is the ruling power in Lamming's Lime Stone, and its influence is felt even in the Isles of the Black Rock. Lamming sardonically gives greater prestige to the House than to Parliament: "People might praise the daring and industry of the nation's parliament; but it was the House which received their ultimate obedience" (p. 13).[9] Ultimately it has been economic considerations that have determined the lives of men; all idealisms and democratic yearnings give place to the greater force of money--a force which is a law unto itself. "No courts could intervene in its decision" (p. 13), the narrator says of this Great House. In the "economy" of Western culture, from mercantilism through capitalism, the marketplace has been preeminent, and through colonization and dominion, humanity has been reduced to a commodity--a valuable "cargo."

The voyage of the ship *Reconnaissance* from Lime Stone to San Cristobal by way of the West Coast of Africa provides the story line. It is a journey "out of time" in that it creates a mythic paradigm from the triangular slave trading route. But this is a journey that will attempt to reverse previous patterns of domination by the House. The ship sails secretly and against the authority of the House of Trade and Justice. Unlike the vessels of previous journeys, the *Reconnaissance* will not pick up slaves on the Guinea coast, and the aim of her commandant is to settle and plant where former adventurers exploited the lands of the New World for their mineral wealth. On the ship's arrival in San Cristobal, all "lawful" booty will be shared among the crew, while the officers (excluding the pilot--a detail we will return to) will jointly own the ship. Finally, and significantly, former patterns of sexual exploitation are to be obviated by the arrangements made to transport a "cargo" of women in the vessel *Penalty*, which will rendezvous with the *Reconnaissance* in San Cristobal.

Such a voyage invites various readings. The ship's attempt to "break loose" not only reflects major phases in Caribbean history, but symbolizes all human efforts to achieve freedom. Imaged in the ship's voyage to self-determination are the ongoing struggles for black emancipation, for women's liberation, for national independence, and for an end to worker exploitation. Telescoping as it does the entire post-Columbian era, the novel calls to account that privileged band of officers and commanders whose repeated new world ventures seem ever to take Western society further away from a promised utopia.

But together with this paradigmatic outward-bound journey of Western progress there is the journey inwards--the middle passage that leads to areas of the self thrust into the shadowy regions of the unconscious, the "Isles of the Black Rock." Each of the officers on board is drawn into confrontation with that Other within the self, symbolized in this novel by the wives and mistresses that the men have abused and now seek to be free from. When they learn that the commandant has arranged for them to meet their womenfolk in San Cristobal, they mutiny, and in fact they never do meet the women. Instead they die, never to be "reborn" since they failed to complete the middle passage journey that alone could be their salvation.

For the enterprise of the *Reconnaissance* ends in failure. Divisions arise between the commandant and his officers, torn as they all are between their utopian vision and the urgent demands of self-interest. In the mutiny that climaxes the undertaking, two officers and the commandant lose their lives, the boatswain goes mad, the ship's cabin boy is transformed into a gun-toting criminal, and the men below decks, led (appropriately) by the

powder maker, lower the boats to take and possess San Cristobal
for themselves. Since the same flaws that doomed the "breaking
loose" led by the commandant are evident in this new generation
of social reformers, there seems little hope that a significantly
"new" order will be established in the New World setting. The
deja vu nature of the whole undertaking is ironically contained
in the ship's name--*Reconnaissance.*

The novel is not entirely without hope, but hope seems to lie
beyond the text. The closing words of the novel, uttered by the
lady of the House, point to this as yet unrealized hope: "We are
a future they must learn," (p. 251), she says. The text of masculine authority--represented in the journals of Master Cecil,
which the commandant uses as his guidebook, the charts and
globes of previous navigators, the journals and amended maps of
the present crew--is revealed by Lamming's narrative strategy to
be bound by its worldview to repetitive patterns of domination
and repression that make for a divided world. The "eye" of the
narrator images four centuries of such history making in a single
mythic voyage that reveals the destructive consequences of
progress as conceived by the West--the "voyage out," the phallic
thrust of technological and economic expansion that has marked
the post-Renaissance period in the Western world. Beyond this
phallocentric "text," though, are the women of the novel's final
section. Imprisoned in a surrealistic, cavelike space that is at
once skull, womb, and tomb, the women deconstruct the histories
of the men. Their voices, however, merely echo in the cave but
are not heard because the men never engage on that voyage
inwards to discover the "other"--the feminine alterity within
themselves. Bent always on new conquests of virgin territories,
they fail to enter the womb from which alone they can be reborn:
the womb of confrontation with "natives" of their own person.

The womblike space that contains the women while their men
sail the high seas climaxes the novel's imagery. It recalls the
"cabin of space" in which the commandant's mistress keeps a
record of her days of suffering and the cabin in which the
commandant himself is haunted by dreams of the woman he
loved and has now lost. It recalls the "womb" of the ship where
carcasses being hacked apart for a feast create a grotesque image
of slaves packed together on shelves in the stinking holds of
trading vessels, making their middle passage by the millions to
the New World where their labor would provide luxury goods for
European consumption. The womb image recalls the repression
of the womenfolk--repression that results in insanity. Steward's
wife is an example. She lives imprisoned in a "wordless solitude"
that has made her room "her fortress and her prison" (p. 210). "I
used to rant and rave like an animal," she confesses. "I would get
a feeling like madness inside me, and there was no one to listen"

(p. 210). The same pattern of repression and confinement that turn into uncontrollable fury is seen in the *cabin* boy, whose innocence is transformed through perpetual deprivation into murderous rage. And finally the womb image recalls the "strategy of the graves": Lamming resorts to legend rather than history when he depicts islanders in the New World, compelled by the first set of Europeans to dig mines (wombs) in their land for the extraction of mineral wealth, preparing for the next arrivals by digging in advance. This time, though, they dig pitlike graves (tombs) for the destruction of the destroyer. The prevailing image in this novel, then, is of womb turned tomb, of lover turned monster, and of a monstrous offspring waiting to be birthed from a cabin of space in which confinement has transformed it into a raging fury.

I propose to focus, then, on the commandant's decision to have a cargo of women waiting in San Cristobal to meet the *Reconnaissance* on its arrival and on the significance of the feminine presence in this novel. Such a feminist reading reveals Lamming's skill in transforming the historical rape of the New World into a myth of man's exploitative interaction with the Other--another race, sex, or class, or indeed the Other as environment or alter ego. By exploring the metaphor of virgin lands that dominated and legitimated the conquest of the New World, we will discover a divided inner psyche writ large upon the landscape--an imposing erection, as it were, that names the Other as feminine--a ruling metaphor that brings with it a variety of consequences.

The women in this novel--all abused, deserted, and maligned by their menfolk--form a collective conscience, an image of that other self from which the men seek to escape. Together with nature herself, they constitute a feminine alterity that has been forsaken by Western ideology. Their voices take over where the male text ceases (both Lamming's text and the journals it engages in parodic dialogue). Just as the voices of the men below decks (slaves and indentured laborers of the sixteenth to nineteenth centuries, exploited labor of the twentiethth) rose in mutiny against the officers "above," so, as the novel closes, the voice of the vast feminine otherness cries out from a womb/tomb in which she is confined.

To the men of the *Reconnaissance* the word (meaning the written word) is primary, "necessary as blood" (p. 19). Indeed, the text of the novel is interspersed with extracts from journals kept by various of the men. Like the accounts in Hakluyt's *Voyages* (Lamming's source for much of the historical detail in this novel), these journals are a curious blend of fact and fiction in which wild fantasies compete for credence with careful scientific observation, pious declarations with arrogant racial slurs, and a fine courage in the face of danger with an uncontrollable lust for gold.

Logocentrism is finely demonstrated in the person of the commandant, whose writing, Ivan the ship's painter comments, "covers more paper than the forest has leaves" (p. 139). To Sasha, the cabin boy, it seems that his master's figure "crouched low over the council table . . . would go on writing forever" (p. 89). It is by means of the written that conquest is made permanent. Boatswain, who has practical experience of the regions the ship sails to, is meek and humbled before the charts and globes that give superior authority to Steward's knowledge.

Knowledge and the written are one and the same in this worldview, and oral tradition counts for nothing. Boatswain deceives himself when he feels that his knowledge of the coast is "worth a fortune in gold" (p. 91); Steward, on the other hand, whose maps were pirated by the man who is now lord treasurer of the House, knows well that it is the man who owns the written word who has authority and power. Even Pierre, the ship's carpenter, unrealistic as he is, can see the relationship between the written and the power to dominate:

A single life is too little time to put on record the   great conversion to knowledge which displaced my former ignorance. For now I did learn to discourse, following the instructions of Steward's learning, how the great globe of the known world was divided up,. . . and by what right and justice the powers and princes hold dominion over what they discover in the continents where science did not yet reach. . . .And believing, as the Scriptures say, that charity should have first birth in a man's native home, I did reckon it a just cause for Lime Stone to claim unto itself whatever fruitful lands might multiply the wealth and glory of our Kingdom, for in the arts of peace and Christian rule we have no equal. (p. 127)

Pierre's words draw together the Word of the Scriptures with the written texts (maps and globes) of an authority that presumes to name the world, revealing the assumed sanctity of the Western worldview. Maps, charts, journals, history--together they are the word of authority that names, and in naming, possesses.

There is, though, in the dialogic world of the novel, a conflict between the word of authority (I) and the reading of that text discovered by the "eye" of the reader. Pious and noble declarations in the journals are belied by words and actions of the men in real life. Pierre's written assertion "In the arts of peace and Christian rule we have no equal" is satirized in the ruthless slaughter by the crew of welcoming natives on the Guinea coast. He declares that "the heathen transported across the ocean seas . . . do rejoice in their new habitation" (p. 128), but the suicide and maroon motifs mutiny against such an idea.

Steward writes of the "new and enlightened society" (p. 31) that they hope to found, but as the narrative proceeds and the corruption of the entire crew becomes evident, that, too, is held up to mockery. Repeatedly, the fictive text responds parodically to the written word of the journals.

Similarly, the personal histories recounted by various of the men to a chosen confidant prove to be fictive constructs whose silences are quickly detected. When Steward, for example, tells how he rescued a young woman from sexual abuse by the lord treasurer and brought her into his own home, he admits that his motives were not entirely altruistic: blackmailing the treasurer would be sweet revenge for the theft by that person of maps Steward had made, and the girl would be a thorn in the flesh to his wife, whose generosity and ambition (on his behalf) have grown irksome to him. What he does not, and indeed could not have related, is that the girl with whom he enjoyed sexual intimacy was in fact his own daughter. Surgeon, listening to the tale, is able to supply this other testimony, for it was he who attended the girl when she died in childbirth.

Steward's wife has yet another "reading" to offer. What Steward had interpreted as love and gratitude in the girl were something else entirely: "The girl was afraid. That is what my eyes forced me to see. How blind he was to this fearful feeling in the girl. Silence was the only service she could offer to save herself. He saw her silence as enjoyment and support. His blindness!" (p. 342).

Steward's story, in fact, encapsulates patterns of domination expressed in this novel through male-female relationships. Leaving his true "wife" for "virgin" lands, he uses the word of his narrative to establish an ideal image of himself and to denigrate his wife. The silences of his text, however, rise up against that I-dentity, revealing another side of Steward, symbolized in the incestuous union. What he had "named" a rescue was a violent assault--and indeed a violent assault on his "own flesh."

The stories of Boatswain and Surgeon follow a similar pattern: both are in flight from women whose virtue so exposes the guilt of their men that it has been renamed lust and powerseeking. About Surgeon's behavior the narrator comments, "If he couldn't come to terms with his own chaos, he would have to create some flaw in her, some lasting deprivation that passion could not remedy" (p. 177).

Their self-destruction, which commenced with the denial of the alter ego within themselves, is mirrored on a larger scale in the sickness of the Demon Coast. Boatswain and others aboard the *Reconnaissance* fall sick with a strange disease that afflicts only the Europeans who sail to the Guinea coast.[10] These men, who declare their intention of bringing Gospel to save the "heathen," do not, in fact, offer communion or brotherhood at all, but instead grow fat on the trade in the black "flesh." In a grotesque parody of the mass, we see Priest and Surgeon engaged in theological discussion, disposing of the "black flesh" as it were, and intermittently sipping wine (Chapter IX). The symbolism reaches a climax during the Christmas (Christ-mass) dinner: "Surgeon . . . had a habit of soaking the dry prunes in his wine; then he would suck for a moment before grazing on the acrid, black flesh" (p. 155). Ironically, though, the curse of the Demon Coast is that those who trade in the black cargoes may end up eating their own flesh--the major symptom of the illness. Thus Lamming's title, *Natives of My Person*, implies a need for humanity to recognize at every level, from the intrapersonal to the international, that the "Other" is a native of the person of the self, and that to deny, repress or colonize that Other is tantamount to autocannibalism.

The process of such colonization begins, as Lamming has indicated, in language, with an arbitrary naming. The wealth, promise, and purity of virgin lands are suggested in the names Guinea Coast and Constance Creek, but other, different, names follow upon the disillusionment experienced by the sailors. The areas become respectively Demon Coast and Creek of Deception. In fact the names are merely a fanciful projection onto reality of the aspirations and fears of the naming person--an externalization of his own self. Thus the Isles of the Black Rock are deprived of the name that gives them equal standing with Lime Stone, and of their mirroring (black/white) character. They are renamed San Cristobal--an expression of the pure and noble aspirations of the men on the *Reconnaissance*. Further, by naming the lands masculine, the invaders implicitly evade confrontation with their own urge to rape--expressed, despite themselves, in their talk of "planting a portion of Lime Stone" in "virgin lands."

Conquest and domination, then, are achieved through politically charged metaphors that ascribe authority to the phallus and the word--a phenomenon that French feminist writers have called "phallologocentrism." It is evident in Surgeon, who has a "lucid vision of himself established in the Isles of the Black Rock, known everywhere as a founder of hospitals, a pioneer in the novel arts of healing" (p. 119). The man disturbs not only with his gross appetite for flesh, but also with his talk of starting "from scratch"--a phrase he keeps repeating--in "virgin lands." Given the virgin-scratch-erection sequence, the suggestion of rape is inescapable. Indeed, his present position is the result of a rape of sorts: he has stolen the medicines with which he will begin his work in the New World and has persuaded his wife (whom he has conveniently had incarcerated in the Severn mental asylum) to bear the blame. Like the other men, Surgeon cannot face the beast within himself, but maintains his "integrity" by naming his wife insane, just as he hopes to win fame by becoming master of

disease through the act of naming it. His wife, wrongly incarcerated and raging helplessly in her confinement, becomes a
symbol for repressed areas of the self and repressed groups of
humankind--both elements that threaten to rise in mutiny and
shatter the "I" that keeps them in bondage.

Steward's mastery of the word and the veiled phallicism in
Surgeon's scientific aspirations combine in the person of the
commandant. And the commandant's mistress, too, is transformed, under his exploitative commodification of her, from
tender virgin to demonic fury. In his dream, she comes to her
lover in a setting rich in nature's bounty:

> He lay full length on the bed and watched the pyramid of fruit
> that rose from the silver platters on the chest. The orchards
> had made their harvest ready for his return. The apples were
> red and fresh as blood. A peach had split open at the stem; she
> must have arranged the peaches in the same crystal bowl his
> mother had used for apples. He saw the delicate udders of the
> pears breathe and swell with sap. A soft, sweet stain of pear
> skin clung to his teeth. He was chewing slowly on the tissue of
> the pear, feeding carefully as a child on the fruits he had seen
> his parents plant. He was learning to eat again. (pp. 60-61)

In this passage, the juxtapositioning of himself as adult and as
child, of mistress and mother, of old world (apples) and virgin
lands (peaches) brings out sharply the masculine conflict
described by Kolodny--of the need for nurturance at the maternal breast and of the desire for individuation through sexual
aggressiveness. Lamming sustains an eerie conflict between the
two: the rape suggested in "red and fresh as blood" and in "split
open at the stem" is countered by the maternal fecundity in
"delicate udders" that "swell with sap."

Wearing "an apple leaf above her hair" (p. 61), the woman
offers fulfillment of the sexuality hinted at in the description of
the fruit as she comes towards him, her gown "opened at her
throat" and coming "apart to her waist" (p. 61). In a deft gesture,
Lamming draws together the mistress and the colonized land:
"She was a colony of joys given over entirely to his care" (p. 65).

But though their bodies are entwined in lovemaking, the
commandant's thoughts are far away, planning how to deal with
the "cannibal" strategies of the tribes:

> There was a treasure of naked flesh in his arms, heaving and
> sobbing like the wind. But he couldn't feel her legs grow tight
> and quivering between his thighs; his desire had taken root
> elsewhere. An imperial joy had shipped his pride over the
> ocean seas. Her breast shook and heaved over his arm. She was
> kneading her hands down the root and testicle of his strength;

his sperm, however, was nurturing a different soil, his star was
ascending a foreign sky. (p. 71)

It is a vivid image of rapacious pirates, absentee landlords, and
modern business undertakings--all plundering, but giving nothing
in return.

At the beginning of their lovemaking, the nibbling and
munching and the reciprocal exploration of each other's body is
a picture of mutual satisfaction. Bus as soon as the mistress
realizes that her lover is absent from her, she changes. Withdrawing from his embrace, she leaves the room and goes to the
solitude of her "cabin of space"--the place where she stores crystal
jars of leaves, each jar representing a voyage, and each leaf a day
of his absence. There she undergoes a transformation, as the
commandant discovers when he comes to speak with her: " An
hour ago she had tamed his hunger with her body .... Now he
could scarcely believe what he was seeing. There was a dangerous stranger lurking behind the terrible calm that came over her
voice and her eyes" (p. 77). His gifts, which hinted ominously that
she was to him merely a harem slave (she had felt "the cold clasp
of the silver hug her throat" (p. 64), and found her throat
"imprisoned" with the splendor of his jewels) now reveal their
true character: she wears the necklace "like a chain of nails" (p.
77). In the tiger's fury that possesses her now that she understands his purpose is to use her and then leave her once again, she
attacks him with a dagger then leaves him alone in a room that
"closed over him like a tomb" (p. 88).

Certain patterns of imagery are present that find an echo in
the response of the tribes to invasion and ruthless exploitation by
the colonizer. Structurally, too, the two are drawn together in
juxtaposition since the commandant's postcoital dream (a dream
within a dream, one remarks) is of tracking down the "cannibal"
tribes with dogs and falling into the pits they had dug to trap
their would-be enslavers. The pits and hollows of the bodies of
the lovers (the "cave" of an ear, the "crater" of her armpit, and
"well" between her breasts) are initially linked with the mines on
the Isles of the Black Rock. Later, though, they take on a more
ominous tone: " The tribes had gone underground, and turned the
earth into a cemetery. At San Souci and Belle Vue the soldiers
slid like worms into their graves. Everywhere. Even before his
arrival, the Tribes had dug graves; and the men under Master
Cecil were buried alive, dying in the dirt, with the dogs their
only company" (p. 70). The womb of delight that the Commandant
seeks becomes an imprisoning tomb, and his desire for nurturance
brings him a "vagina dentata" and the threat of being consumed.

The problem appears to be one of reification. The mistress,
like the Isles, has been named a colony, and the man a commandant; the text gives them no personal names. He is unable to

perceive the Other within himself: "he remained forever unaware of any guilt that might attach to his actions" (p. 76).[11] Nor can he conceive of his mistress as anything other than a colony existing for his "imperial joy." Her body is beautiful and sexually satisfying, but their relationship is limited to the physical; his silence--that is, his refusal to communicate with her as an intelligent individual with emotional needs of her own --is what transforms her into a fury, "silent on her face, chewing the sheets, and digging her nails without a sound through the wet groves of her hair" (p. 67). Unwilling to face the charges of "butcher" and "human-eater" with which she confronts him, the commandant escapes from her and from the "sinister labyrinth" (p. 87) into which her reasoning would draw him. Her deprivation mirrors that of the women of the tribes: "But she had never known the curse of toil enforced on her waiting. She had seen the women of the Tribes go in droves, herded like cattle across the farms, digging the earth with sticks and naked hands" (p. 84).

The commandant too engages in self-mutilation: "he was chewing his lips, ploughing up the heavy shrub of eyebrow with his thumb" (p. 66); "his nails were digging quietly at his thighs" (p. 84); "his nails were making a chart of rivers down his thighs" (p. 84). With the words "ploughing," "digging" and "chart" Lamming links the commandant's exploitative, possessive interaction with the Other with a compulsive abuse of his own body. Ivan, the painter, who reflects the landscape dominated by imperialism, reveals its wounds in his face: "His skin was spidery with lines like a chart of veins and scars all over his face" (p. 49). Here the outer cosmos is seen as a vast mirror of the inner: each reification of the Other, each refusal to encounter the Other within the self, leads to antagonism between self and Other which is, in effect, a destructive division of the person.

We have seen the virgin lands metaphor at work in several ways. Virgin purity in the land and womenfolk mirrors the noble idealism of the men. Its counterpart, the denial of man's sexual and materialistic rapacity, emerges as a projection onto the feminine Other of the image of "whore." Whoredom, says the lady of the House, is the "national principle" (p. 349) of Lime Stone, and the private vices of citizens have been made "the nation's religion" (p. 349). Indeed, whoredom in this novel is given considerable metaphoric weight. It names not only, as I have demonstrated, the projection onto another of repressed guilty areas in one's person, but also the degeneration of all human intercourse to the level of mere economic exchange. The commodification of mankind into cargoes speaks volubly not only of the Atlantic slave trade, horrific as that was, but also of a wider reification that continues its oppression in subtler ways.

Another dimension of the virgin lands metaphor is found in the fear of a monstrous birth, imaged clearly in the eruption from her womblike "cabin of space" of the commandant's wife transformed into a "tiger's fury." "What a seed the kingdom planted" (p. 47), muses Baptiste, the powder maker, as he relates to the men the story of his father's revenge on the bishop who raped his wife (Baptiste's mother). "He just turned wild like the dogs in the North" (p. 47). Another monstrous birth is witnessed when Sasha, an innocent child at the outset of the voyage, emerges from the commandant's cabin and from his own condition of slavery transformed into a criminal, a murderer.

Despite such fears, the male text persists in naming the Other a fertile womb to be enjoyed. Below decks in the "belly" of the ship, cooks prepare a feast for the officers above. Here it is the working classes who are presented as a feminine Other brutally raped for the gratification of a few:

> It was dark and sweating down below. The heat grew like a fever in the belly of the ship. The cooks were busy severing two dry, stiff carcasses, hooked and swinging from a wet rod of iron overhead. The sweat ran like oil down their necks. They fought with axe and saw, cleaving and drilling through the splinters of bone. The smoked meat was bleeding some nameless substance over their hands. Here, in this echoing hollow of the ship now moist with heat and the smell of wombs, they hacked and parried with their tools, carving up huge rations of meat. (p. 229)

The image of human society presented in this passage is startling and dramatic. There is brutality (cleaving, drilling, hacked, and parried) on the one hand, and indescribable suffering on the other (fever, sweat, "bleeding some nameless substance"). The total impression is of an incestuous rape--the material, nourishing womb brutally plundered to satisfy gross, unrestrained appetites.

Since what has been named virgin in fact includes males, castration images also abound. Sasha, the cabin boy, is dressed in feminine clothing and has a "woman's voice" (p. 89). A hint of homosexual rape comes across in the mention of his being allowed to sleep in the commandant's bed (p. 60). The removal of the men from the women of the tribes is itself an act of castration, and their "digging the earth with sticks and naked hands" is charged with the sexual frustration of the Commandant's mistress "digging her nails . . . through the groves of her hair" (p. 67).

The great, castlelike ship, with masts and guns and its all-male crew of chart makers and history writer, is, then, a fine image of Western culture, dominated by the phallus and the word. Its defiant thrust is forever toward the future: "borne from wave to wave, faring . . . forward" (p. 19), and memory of the past is rejected as an impediment to the enterprise. Mastery of nature through knowledge is, in fact, one of the main themes in this novel. To name the vast otherness is to possess and conquer it--so the journals and charts would imply.

Indeed, knowledge of the Other is repeatedly presented as having degenerated into a means to power or economic asset. The confidants to whom Steward, Surgeon, and Boatswain relate their stories are immediately feared by the three as having dangerous power. Duclos, too, relates that he is in the commandant's power because the commandant knows his personal history (p. 141). Sasha, observing the men around him, embarks on a "new pursuit of learning" (p. 213): he develops a "habit of collecting views" (p. 212), and with his secret store of knowledge begins to "feel the power that secret knowing conferred on older people" (p. 212). When Priest realizes that the commandant knows his personal history, he is aware, too, that such knowledge "could be made lethal as any weapon of war" (p. 269). Bribery and blackmail, violence and insanity are the inevitable concomitants of such a pursuit of knowledge as power. "Tell them," yells the crazed Boatswain, "that I was a man of many parts" (p. 268). But sadly he communicates the distress of the person raped by the knowing eye of another: "People remember what happened only as a way of diminishing the man who made it happen. I say: listen to me; but all hearing is cut short by superior explanation" (p. 268).

Around him, the natural world withdraws from the rape of a man's gaze: "His eyes wandered everywhere, eager to learn the meaning of these objects that slipped into hiding at the slightest intrusion from his glance" (p. 268). Boatswain, though, is unable to protect himself from the vast eye that swallows him: "He was alarmed by the power of the sun that held him there, gazing without sight into its eye" (p. 267). The walls of the self, the very boundaries that define the person, depend on a meeting of I and eye. Retreat into one's cabin of space away from the brutal rape of being seen by the other leads to insanity and death; exposure to that rape is death of another kind, reducing the self to a perpetual object making possible another's subjectivity.

Of withdrawal of nature from the intrusive, penetrative activity of the empirical method, Heidegger says, "Earth thus shatters every attempt to penetrate into it. It causes every merely calculating importunity upon it to turn into a destruction."[12] The kind of withdrawal Heidegger describes is a recurrent motif in *Natives*. We have seen the commandant's mistress withdrawing from his exclusively sexual embrace and being transformed in his dreaming perception of her into a wild beast. Physical nature, too, is presented initially as a loving mistress to be wooed: "The tide quickened and came high up the bow, rubbing its weight against the waist of the ship" (p. 10). But although she will be wooed, she will not be forced, and the inviting embrace becomes, before long, confinement in a clammy tomb as fog "buries" the ship: "One morning the men stood aghast on the decks as they

watched the masts and sails disappear in a thick shroud of mist
and fog. The winds grew more feeble every hour, until they
finally died away . . . . The men grew fearful of this zone of
ocean which seemed to disrupt the regular course of nature" (p.
59). The pattern is repeated in the mines turned graves on the
Isles of the Black Rock and when what began as praise of virgin
lands ends with a vision of the island of Dolores (aptly named)
rising "like an enormous tomb" (p. 294) from the ocean. Throughout, Lamming portrays nature as bountiful in favors but possessing a treacherous character when abused.

The knowledge sought by such as Steward, with his charts and
maps, is the means to material mastery; he is, as Marcel observes
in his journal, "keeper of all the ocean's charts" (p. 38). Such
material conquest, though, as Marcel has also experienced (when
he was handed over "like a box of cargo" (p.39) in exchange for
black slaves), leads to humanity's reification. An alternative
mode of knowing--almost a model of Buber's I-Thou or of
Heidegger's reflection upon the essence of the Thing--is presented
in the person of Marcel the fisherman. Marcel's interaction with
the Other takes the form of a meditative communion: "The
fisherman was leaning against the rib of the ship, meditating on
the heave and swell of the sea. He saw a huge mackerel surface
and briefly float before diving out of sight; and his eyes grew
gentle. His gaze was soft, almost affectionate in its concentration
on the water . . .;the fisherman seemed . . . lost in wonder" (p. 36).
Pointing out a fish in the water, Marcel tells Baptiste, "It's a holy
feeling for the night to catch you out in that dark, just you and
a population larger than all Lime Stone swimming deep under
and around your boat" (p. 143). Marcel's communion with the sea
ushers in a moment of lyrical harmony that is reflected in
nature's embrace: "There was a blaze of starlight. The new moon
was coming up over a purple hump of cloud, kissing the water
with its shadow. They . . . watched how the river was combing
the drowned reflection of the moon, dancing and waving like a
woman's hair over the body of the fish" (pp. 144-145). Marcel's
interaction with the sea is of subject with subject--standing in
sharp contrast with the attitude of mastery and control to some
further purpose that characterizes the interaction of the officers.
It is not without significance that Marcel is remarkable for his
inner composure: "Slow and casual, with an infinite sense of
freedom in everything he did" (p. 32).

Marcel, "castrated" during his captivity (he had his ear cut
off), with his "widow's peak," and in his association with the
moon, is evidently a man who has accepted the feminine in
himself. So is Ivan, the painter. And both are men of vision.
Ivan depicts the kind of knowledge that is mystic and intuitive.
Illiterate, he has been introduced to the "mysteries" of the faith
"through the fabulous pictures of saints and angels" (p. 29). His

convictions rest not on empirical foundations, but "on a different kind of evidence" (p. 28), not on the word, but on the associative power of images. Ivan confesses the "mystery" in nature that forever lies beyond our empirical grasp, our exploitative material analysis. He has desired to enter the Church "to be let into the mysteries" (p. 50), and despite Pierre's mockery, asserts that "there's more in these ocean seas than ordinary intellect can catch" (p. 50); "there's a kind of knowledge which doesn't need every truth. Just a few and deep" (p. 51).

Characteristically reflective, Ivan is always associated with the feminine. The vision that he has toward the end of the voyage is linked with the night, the moon, and a (womb like) tunnel of earth in which are "blades of corn . . . and blossoming seeds of pepper" (p. 239). Overhead an unusually large moon further emphasizes the novel's motif of the mutiny of a repressed feminine against a dominant, masculine world represented in the ship. Ivan's vision is of the lady of the House, standing on a cliff. In one hand she holds a jar of leaves looking alternately like wine and like blood; in the other she holds the ship (p. 243). The leaves kept by the lady in her crystal jar are a silent witness, corresponding leaf for leaf with the pages of the commandant's text. Each leaf describes a pain-filled, blood-stained "other" reading of the historic "voyage" of Western civilization. The wine enjoyed by the few "above decks" is the transubstantiated blood of the silent millions kept in confinement "below" and "in the dark." And in fact the ship has gone nowhere; it has never moved from the lady's hand. She is not only a grotesquely parodic figure of liberty but also an Old World figure of justice--the *Penalty* is still to come. Images erupt from the silent interstices speaking more volubly than countless pages of authority's text.

A silent, feminine Other, then, is in constant mutiny against confinement in the naming of a masculine text. As the ship approaches the Guinea coast, scene of ruthless deportation (castration) of the menfolk of the tribes, an omen occurs. Magnificently plumaged birds dive toward the ship, committing mass suicide in the rigging and on the decks of the ship (p. 104). It takes hours for the men to clean the decks of the broken bodies which, are greedily consumed by crocodiles. The scene of carnage lingers, though, as does the chilling memory of the incident: "The sunlight poured like rain over the glistening acres of carnage that covered the mouth of the river" (p. 105). This suicide of birds symbolizes that of the slaves who, according to Pierre's journal, being "not adequate in the powers of reason . . . did make a leap overboard in the night" (p. 111). Like the carcasses of the birds, their bodies proved (again according to Pierre) a "great inconvenience" (p. 111), impeding the ship's progress upriver to obtain replacements for the wasted cargo!

The leap of the slaves and the plunge of the birds are linked, too, with rumor of suicide by tribes folk in the islands (p. 99).

Materially it is the ones who die who are victims, but the incident takes on profound psychological significance as members of the crew betray how deeply they have been disturbed by the incident. Speaking of rumors that suicides have occurred among the islanders, Boatswain complains, "They were a stubborn breed, making a joke of suicide, killing themselves to make a mockery of our conquest" (p. 99). In juxtaposing history and rumor, Lamming's narrative strategy proves, once again, a deconstruction of European text. Using these silent spaces in historical account, Lamming transforms victims into heroes and despair into triumph. The conqueror, conversely, is mocked, deprived of his victory: it is he who is now named the "marooned" one (p. 104), and his imposing "craft" is left in tatters: "Boatswain . . . considered the chaos below. There was a great tangle of rope everywhere. A small lateen sail had been torn from its cordage. The ensigns had fallen from the masthead, and the ragged tatters of a banner were floating over the plucked white feathers of the sea fowl" (p. 104).

Finally, nature herself joins with memory, conscience, the poor, and the oppressed, constantly invading the peace of mind of the oppressor:

> The river was everywhere. Green precipices of leaves splintered and fell amidst the turbulent screams that rose from the decks . . . . The black cargoes of flesh were slowly borne away; but the coast shook and trembled as a giant stride of sound made a fury of wailing through the forest. It seemed the trees were about to make sacrifices, as each leaf and branch tottered before the sudden crush of a gale. The wind went mad. There was a throttled murmur of drums echoing from afar. (p. 129)

Throughout the novel, sea and river, wind and sun, the moon, illness, bees and birdsong (or absence of it) join forces to become a vast, wordless yet eloquent power--a "chorus" of wholly other--that asserts itself against the historic enterprise. This autochthonous power mutinies against the ego-bound authority represented in the ship: "There was a fretful wind coming off the river. Baptiste reflected: was reflecting, as though the black coast had driven him forever inward. This weight of self-inquiry had become his habit, his way of being" (p. 131). Boatswain, also driven by the carnage around him to reflection on his relationship with the lady, is invaded by nature. Bees start humming in his ear, and the sea roars in his head; the sun sends bullets toward him, and the church bells of Aberlon where he murdered his mistress haunt his memory. The law of nature is that when the Other within the self is repressed, that Other rises in mutiny, bringing shipwreck to the ego-bound self.

Man alone lives in a divided world, for nature herself is One. Lamming depicts ature as a multiform whole. The land is present in the sea, the sea in the land, the past lies within the present and present informs the past, bells and birds invade the minds of men at sea and the surge of the tide fills their thoughts on land, the colonies are within the kingdom, and the kingdom within the colonies. When this essential oneness and interrelatedness of reality is denied and nature viewed through the distorting frame of man's divided psyche, then the monsters are created. Reciprocity and community will be achieved only when man steps outside of the metaphor that denies his essentially "androgynous" nature.

Lamming's criticism of the Western method of dividing the land into saleable portions was introduced in *Castle*, through the anxious response of villagers to the arbitrary sale of their ancestral lands. In *Natives*, the Western method of carving up the land (imaged in Steward's charts and globes and reflected in Ivan's ravaged face) and of reducing human beings to cargoes of marketable commodities acquires far more sinister overtones. The violent imagery of cannibalism and dismemberment, of self-mutilation and of insanity makes the point that the unrestrained destruction of the Other (including the environment) is, in fact, self-destruction. In their cave, the women are in limbo, suspended between life (womb) and death (tomb). The release of this feminine Other--without which man will not be reborn--will require a new kind of "knowing." As the lady says, "We are a future they must learn" (p. 351).

For the dream-metaphor that can offer hope certainly lies outside, beyond, the House that Western civilization has built for itself--the Great House that names the rest of the world a plantation to be exploited perpetually. The West, like Surgeon, has made itself the indispensable consumer. Surgeon's eating, we read, "was a kind of performance in which he saw himself in many roles. Exclusive and indispensable. It was as though he existed in order to give food some useful purpose. He embodied all forms of appetite" (p. 156).

It is curious to notice how the officers aboard the *Reconnaissance* portray the various dominion metaphors detailed by Ms. Merchant in her study. Steward is the custodian; Surgeon the one who probes and analyzes in order to control; the commandant seeks to plant a portion of Lime Stone in "virgin" lands; and Priest provides the rhetoric that gives the enterprise a noble coloring. A "forced union" can be "made holy" (p. 249) only by his peculiar gift.

It remains to discuss Pinteados, the ship's pilot, and perhaps the most intriguing of the characters in *Natives of My Person*. Lamming takes the figure from Hakluyt. Pinteados appears in

Richard Eden's account of an actual expedition in 1553 under
Captain Wyndham to Guinea and Benin. Eden tells of

a stranger called Anthony Anes Pinteado,[13] a Portugal born in
a town named the port of Portugal, a wise, discreet and sober
man, who for his cunning in sailing, being as well an expert
pilot as a politic captain, was sometime in great favor with the
King of Portugal, and to whom the coasts of Brazil and Guinea
were committed to be kept from the Frenchmen, to whom he
was a terror on the sea in those parts, and was furthermore a
gentleman of the King his master's house.[14]

Fallen on adversity, though, Pinteados came to England and
sailed as cocaptain with Wyndham. However, says Eden, "in this
golden voyage he was evil matched with an unequal companion,
an unlike match of most sundry qualities and conditions, with
virtues few or none adorned."[15] Wyndham apparently reduced
Pinteados to the status of a common mariner, assuming sole
command. Although Pinteados had been repeatedly humiliated
by Wyndham, when the captain died of a mysterious sickness that
was decimating the crew, Pinteados lamented "as if he had been
the dearest friend he had in the world."[16] Even then the man's
troubles were not over, for the crew mutinied against Pinteados,
reducing him to the status of ship's boy. Days later, Pinteados
died, "for very pensiveness and thought that struck him to the
heart; a man worthy to serve any prince, and most vilely used."[17]
    Eden's account concludes with two letters written by the King
of Portugal and the Infante his brother, clearing Pinteados of the
false charges that had driven him to England and offering him
a stipend. Apparently Pinteados felt that despite such letters it
would be dangerous for him to return home.
    Evidently Lamming found this story a rich ground for his
imagination. It provided him with his themes of misrepresenta-
tion and mutiny, of intrigue and betrayal, of the assertion of a
dominant "I" in a power struggle that meets its nemesis in the
form of a mysterious sickness that decimates the crew. But
chiefly, Pinteados--skilled craftsman hounded into exile and pilot
of the "middle passage"--provides Lamming's text with a figure
of the artist as novelist. It is Pinteados who brings together the
crew and arranges the rendezvous with the Penalty's cargo of
women. Without Pinteados, the ship cannot sail. Silent witness
of all that occurs, it is he who initiates the middle passage each
of the officers embarks on--the journey inward to hidden areas
of the self. When the voyage is over, it is Pinteados who ties up
loose ends, reporting to Badaloza the outcome of the venture.
Unlike Eden's scapegoat figure, Lamming's Pinteados, trickster-
like, evades any sacrificial role, mirroring those around him but
himself "seen" and mirrored by no one. Pinteados's craft, like

Lamming's, is twofold: his literal voyage is akin to the novelist's
plot line; his initiation of the officers' rite of passage is akin to
the silent resonances in the interstices of the plot line--imagery,
resonant juxtaposition, echoes in the text, and parody. The text
itself is both masculine and feminine, active and reflective,
moving forward and backward in time.

Pinteados, then, is both an "I" and an "eye." As eye he lives
outside the history-making process that established the "I" in
Western terms. Unlike Steward, who decides he "would enter
history through the permanence of stone; and . . . marveled at the
way time could fix a name" (p. 202), Pinteados despises the notion
that man is the sum of his material achievements. When he enters
the room of Admiral Badaloza with its "treasure of heroic faces"
(p. 327) framed on the walls, he realizes anew that "he did not
want to sojourn here" (p. 327). Even on arrival at the Admiral's
quarters, he had symbolically expressed his contempt for the
assumed sanctity of that "House" in a gesture that places dirt
back in the sanctuary:[18] "He kicked a patch of dirt over the
threshold of the door; then paused, admiring the blue curve of
the bay" (p. 326).[19]

For it is only by stepping *outside history*--history conceived of
as a record of heroic conquest of the material world--that
Pinteados can attain the essential being he seeks: "His native
Antarctica was a name; its history was a label that was no longer
relevant to this creation of himself as the absolute foreigner" (p.
326). Such a state of exile (liminality) grants Pinteados the
license of the fool--a freedom not experienced by men within the
boundaries and under the dictatorship of ideologies. Asked by
Admiral Badaloza which way his path now lay, the pilot replies:
"Everywhere and in any zone" (p. 328); he is, the narrator
comments, "resolute about his multiple choice of direction" (p.
328). Like Anancy on his web, he opts for the freedom of the
crossroads.

Refusing to be in bondage to any ideological investment or
political commitment and preferring instead the honesty and
integrity that requires an ongoing reflection upon reality,
Pinteados is the stranger on board; the eye amidst I's intent on
creating themselves through action. Indeed, the men are disturbed by the oppressive silence of their pilot, and have a fearful
respect for his capacity to see. They speak of his "good eye," his
"fast eye," his "clear eye" (pp. 19-20), and complain that "He
doesn't spare a word that would help you see inside him. Keeps
everything tight shut" (p. 19). Again, the strategy for survival in
a world that seeks to penetrate the self in invasive and manipula-
tive ways is the retreat into the masking "castle" of one's skin
from which one can observe, reflectively, while remaining
unseen.

Pinteados's decision to create himself by choosing to withdraw from the material evaluation of penetrating "eyes" and stepping outside of the history metaphor altogether is one of the key differences between himself and Ivan. Ivan remains very close to society and its political issues. He enters into a "sacred partnership" with the revolutionary powder maker, Baptiste. "The plan had become an absolute necessity for the fulfillment of the painter's vision" (p. 310). For Lamming, political engagement and artistic vision are inseparable, the one implying the other. But although Pinteados is in exile, his weaving of events serves, just as does Ivan's vision, to achieve social change, as Baptiste recognizes. Baptiste says: "I would have it known . . . that there be one man among the officers who at this time venture to give us benefit of his knowledge. It was Pinteados, the pilot, a foreigner whose conduct in the entire business we cannot fathom . . . . Believing him to be the least in importance in our business, it so happened he intervened in a way most suited to our interests" (p. 316). Together, Ivan, illiterate representative of the artist in the oral tradition, and Pinteados--presenting the folk cause in written form, and thus doubly exiled from his people--portray the artist in the Caribbean in his various conflicts.

With the issue of literacy, the notion of exile takes on yet another dimension. Like G and Chiki, Pinteados is removed from the folk by his literacy, yet remains a stranger to the officers because of his foreignness. Containing in himself the folk tradition and Western cultural heritage, he stands between the two worlds, in exile from both, yet promoting dialogue between them. His position is one of painful "crucifixion," yet also of power. He reflects the bastard fatherless child, the divided self of the West Indian, but transforms his deprivation into possibility.

Unconcerned with events in time--"he showed no interest in the substance of any report which the Admiral might prepare" (p. 321)--he probes beneath the surface of linear narratives of history to the silences they reveal. He takes the fictive construct of the I-author, that narrative thread of history, and the empty silent spaces of its omissions. In this plurality of discourse that is his web, Pinteados-Anancy provides a divining text in which Mr. Hate-to-Be-Contradicted can see what a contradiction he himself is, and how destructive his fictions are.

Lamming's portrayal of Pinteados, the shaman-pilot of the middle passage, as "absolute foreigner" serves as a pertinent transition to a discussion of Harris. For it is Harris's insistence on such absolute condition of exile that sets him apart from a contemporary Caribbean emphasis on African roots.[20] Critics such as E. K. Brathwaite, Gordon Rohlehr, and Sylvia Wynter are currently exploring African elements that inspire art in the Caribbean in such works as Edward Brathwaite's seminal essay "The African Presence in Caribbean Literature," Gordon Rohlehr's recent full-length study of Brathwaite's poetry and a number of articles on calypso, and Sylvia Wynter's "Jonkonnu in Jamaica." Harris, by contrast, resists homogeneity in any form, African or otherwise, insisting that the ground of creative potential in the West Indies lies in a cultural heterogeneity. Potential growth points in a diversified Caribbean cultural landscape, he believes, are the crossroads where various cultures meet.

A state of exile is "native ... to the Caribbean poet"[21] because the West Indian poet is always a stranger to any single, or culturally monistic standpoint. For Harris, West Indian philistinism consists in the region's "refusal to perceive its own dismembered psychical world."[22] Hence for the poet to adopt the viewpoint of either House or folk is ultimately for him to commit the identical error of omission, for either viewpoint merely confirms the framing duality marked by House/folk. Outside a polarized world, beyond ideologies of conquest and protest, the trickster-artist finds a "profound exile," becomes a "womb of space," to use Harris's formulation.

Harris's project is to reveal crossroads as sites of rich potential where cultures meet. He conceives the artist as one who takes the perceptions of texts of authority and explains their silences with deconstructive energy until such silences are "subtly redressed within the cross-cultural web, subtly enriched within and against other apparently alien imaginations which gain also in themselves and in their works by re-visionary interpretations that they too undergo in cross-cultural context."[23] Harris's quoted words refer to dialogue among literary works, but they invite a social reading.

Harris believes that cultures tend to become "enmeshed in codes to invert or overturn each other rather than become involved in complex mutuality and the difficult creation of community."[24] Hence Harris construes identity, whether personal or national, as a potentially alienating destructive construct. It represents a definition of the self that depends on a system of polarizing oppositions and hierarchizations such as House/folk. A quest for community, in contrast, is an attempt to move beyond social structures of hierarchy to a oneness in which interrelatedness and interdependence take precedence over differences.[25] Harris would, by inference, designate the current quest for an African identity in the Caribbean as counter to his personal vision of heterogeneous community.

In *Palace of the Peacock* (1960), Harris's first novel, a multiracial, all-male crew makes a boat journey upriver into the Guyanese hinterland to obtain cheap labor for the coastal estate of Donne, leader of the expedition. The craft arrives at Mariella, an Amerindian mission, only to find that the folk have run away to avoid capture. Forcing an old Arawak woman to act as their guide, Donne insists that they pursue the fleeing tribes folk--a decision that leads to disaster. The entire crew is lost. The novel ends, though, not with catastrophe, but with the men "climbing" a waterfall to a vantage point above the stream they had foundered in all their lives. From the "eye and window" (p. 144) through which they then see the "repetitive boat and prison" (p. 104) of their material existence, they experience a vision of wholeness that exposes former realities as mere "chains of illusion" (p. 151). The "community" that the men finally enjoy is a sacramental moment communicated through images of music and dance.

Like that of the *Reconnaissance*, the voyage of Donne's unnamed ship is a palimpsest of Caribbean history, and the violence and greed, the cruelty and lust of the crew recall the generations of a blood-stained history that has left deep scars in the Caribbean imagination. The narrative invokes the prehistoric arrival of the Indians as well as of sixteenth- and seventeenth-century conquistadors of every European nation. Fugitive folk recall runaway Indians, escaped slaves, abused women, and brutalized nature alike. Abundant references to gold call to mind the El Dorado legend that once lured adventurers like Sir Walter Raleigh to their death, and still draws pork-knockers, government officials, and foreign investors alike to brave the danger of flood, snakes, and sickness in order to survey hidden but golden prospects. All of the ideological ventures of history seem to have ended in catastrophe. But out of this brokenness, Harris believes, hope may come of a new redeeming world vision. For the melting pot in which the "base" metals' ideological commitment lose their identity make possible the alchemical discovery of the philosopher's stone, the talismanic rock on which a new community may be founded.

In *Palace* Harris draws on pre-Columbian myth for his motif of the "magical corpse." In this myth, Harris explains, the hero clings to a bridge over a stream and looks at the stream but never immerses himself. Should he fall, he would be "immersed once more in the peculiar fabric of creation which has its contradictions and irrationalities."[26] Removed from the stream, though, in a reflective rather than an active pose, the hero acquired new vision: "lucidity ... drawn from his spectatorial powers."[27] In the stream (the flow of historical time and human action), perception structures a polarized world in an attempt to order the "contradictions and irrationalities" of an apparently chaotic reality. There are, though, lucid moments of reflection where the historical "I" turns "eye," dying, as it were, to the world of action, but becoming a womb of light reflecting on the wholeness of reality from a position of exile--a spiritual vantage point.

This movement in and out of the stream is repeated not only in the culminating vision of Harris's novel, but also in various

"deaths" of crew members as they journey up river. A dialectic
is established between technological craft (the boat) and limbo
musing (on the spidery ladders of the cliff face), so that together
they offer a fine metaphor for the dialectical processes of the
creative imagination as it first structures a worldview and then
steps outside in a deconstructive revision of former premises. To
employ a Gestalt model, one might say that an African revival
challenges the preeminence of the white vase, privileging instead
the black faces of a backgrounded folk. Harris, however, carries
us beyond the Gestalt. He insists that the artist be an "absolute
foreigner" to the entire model: that he shatter both vase and
faces in order to achieve an altogether new metaphor.

So we see that *Palace* is about perception--about the limited
and partial perceptions of men caught in ideological structures,
and about the creative vision that is birthed out of exile beyond
ideological investments. The novel is a rite of passage into
community--an invitation, a revealing of sacra, a journey inward
to vision. Seeing is a theme established in the first chapter. The
narrator, half brother to Donne (that is to say, his alter ego),
begins his narrative with the words "I dreamt I awoke with one
dead seeing eye and one living closed eye." As he and Donne look
out through the window in the room, they look "through Donne's
dead seeing material eye rather than through the narrator's living
closed spiritual eye" (p. 14). Donne (his name suggests that he is
concerned only with the material and historical--with what is
done; and also that he has a "metaphysical" dimension invoked
through association with John Donne, the English poet) has
elected to keep his spiritual eye closed. His nameless brother
(that is, his bracketed, negated other self) is, in contrast, a
dreamer. The narrator confesses that in the material world that
Donne rules, he is blind: "you were the one who saw, and I was
the one who was blind" (p. 18). Nevertheless, the musing dreamer
"sees" what Donne is blind to; he "stared blindly through the
window at an invisible population" (p. 17).

Donne and his crew live their lives in the stream, in forward
moving action, unlike the I-narrator, who has become a passive
"eye," musing reflectively upon historical events. The crew is
concerned with material conquest: "Rule the land . . . [and] you
rule the world" (p. 19), is Donne's motto. Their "craft," with its
paddles, its propeller, its engine, defies the powers of nature,
appearing "like a shell after an ecstasy of roaring water and of
fast rocks . . . where the foam forced its way and seethed and
curdled and rushed" (p. 22). Denying this shell-like frailty, they
assert their phallic energies. Their bow "poked the bushy fringe
on the bank" (p. 26) and, "armed . . . with prospecting knives" (p.
26), they force their way through "leafy curtains . . . and masks
of living beard" of the forest (p. 26) like rapists of the land.

To Donne, landscape and people alike are economic resources

to be exploited: "All names of regions were economic names to command and choose from (as one chose to order one's labouring folk around) .... They knew he had once dreamt of ruling them with a rod or iron and a ration of rum" (pp. 84-85). Women--like the land--exist, in Donne's mind, only for man's profit. The folk will "lead us home safely," he assures his crew, "and we'll cultivate our fields and our wives" (p. 104). He looks upon his Amerindian mistress--whose name (Mariella) is the same as that of the land she lives on--"as at a ... senseless creature whom he governed and ruled like a fowl" (p. 15). Even Cameron, jovial as he is, has the same exploitative attitude: "If only the right understanding missy and mistress would come along sweet and lucky, Bucky and rich, 'Ah would be in heaven, boys'" (p. 43), he confides to the others.

As in Lamming's *Natives*, such an assault on nature is not without its penalty. When the crew enter the forest, an eerie sound is heard: "A sigh swept out of the gloom of the trees, unlike any human sound as a mask is unlike flesh and blood. The unearthly, half-gentle, half-shuddering whisper ran along the tips of graven leaves. Nothing appeared to stir. And then the whole forest quivered and sighed and shook with violent instantaneous relief in a throaty clamour of waters as we approached the river again" (pp. 26-27).

The narrator, terror-stricken by this "sigh and ubiquitous step" (p. 28), finds that he is no longer the hunter but the hunted, and gives out a "loud ambushed cry" (p. 28). Mariella, too, (embodying the land in her person) eventually can no longer tolerate the cruel treatment Donne metes out, and (so the narrator dreams) becomes a "wild demon" (p. 16) and an "enigma" (p. 24), shooting down the man who has abused her. In similar fashion, the folk, as Donne gives chase, only retreat further away, so that the narrator is "struck by a peculiar feeling of absence of living persons in the savannas where Donne governed" (p. 24). For in his determination to conquer and crush, Donne has succeeded only in "annihilating everyone and devouring himself in turn" (p. 24). Arriving at Mariella to seize laborers, the men dream themselves "devoured" (p. 37) by canoes. Donne is still to learn the truth in what Schomberg says to Cameron: "Maybe you don't understand you can drive and scare the blasted soul of the world away and lose your bait for good" (pp. 43-44).

As in Lamming's *Natives*, the pattern emerges of nature as womb turned tomb in response to a "rape" perpetrated as a penetrative act of violence and power. But where Lamming's vision is of barrenness and destruction consequent on the rampant materialism of the West and its violent invasion of other cultures, Harris's is of the possibilities born even out of such catastrophe. The recurring dance step of this novel is a sequence in which appearances of nightmare and death are transformed into visions of pattern, beauty, and splendor. This type of transforming vision occurs, for example, when the crew settle down one night in their makeshift camp and the narrator slips into a dream of Donne, his brother. His "musing re-enactment and reconstruction of the death of Donne" (p. 46) seems to symbolize the futile emptiness of the conqueror's ventures. Colors of daylight fade into a landscape of black and white shapes created by the campfire casting its dimly red light on hammocks strung among the trees.   To the narrator, every hammock appears transformed into "an empty cocoon as hollow as a deserted shell and a house" (p. 45). He becomes aware of the absence of true life in the empty forms of material existence-- "fire devoid of all burning spirit" (p. 46). Into this desolate scene comes a vision of death, "half-wolf, half-donkey, monstrous, disconsolate" (p. 46), and the narrator sits up in sudden terror, "a dead man in his bed come to an involuntary climax" (p. 46). Grey shades, "empty" hollow (i.e., womblike) forms, monstrous threat, and wet dream combine in the brother's nightmare to communicate a particularly tragic and barren vision of reality. But with morning comes an alchemical transformation as the sun rises and tragic polarizations yield to a vision of design: "A pearl and half-light and arrow shot along the still veined branches. The charcoal memory of the hour lifted as a curtain rises upon the light of an eternal design" (p. 47).   The narrator confesses the "enormous frailty" (p. 47) of his perceptions, realizing that consciousness itself is "but another glimmering shadow hedging the vision and the glory and the light" (p. 48).

   The occurrence of transforming visions such as the brother's reaches its culmination in the novel's visionary finale as the craft (of ideological commitment) is finally wrecked at the foot of a waterfall, and the crew climb out of the stream, making their ascent by way of a spider-web ladder on the face of the fall. In a sequence of visionary experiences, they at last discover the "true substance of life" and enter into oneness and communitas, symbolized by dance, music, and rainbow colors. The place is the palace of the peacock, whose countless eyes represent a plurality of perspectives and mutual reflection that is the nearest humanity can come to true vision.

   The crew's journey through repeated deaths and repeated rebirths takes place under the shamanistic tutelage of an Arawak woman, the muse and spirit of the land. Indistinguishable from the land itself, she appears "old and wrinkled . . . still as a bowing statue" (p. 71), yet is also "fantastically young and desirable" (p. 75), with her hair "all flowing back upon them with silent streaming magesty and abnormal youth and in a wave of freedom and strength" (p. 73). Her oneness with the landscape emerges in the following passage: "Tiny embroideries resembling the handwork on the Arawak woman's kerchief and the wrinkles on her brow turned to incredible and fast soundless breakers of foam. Her crumpled bosom and river grew agitated with desire, bottling and shaking every fear and inhibition and outcry" (p. 73).

The old woman, musing on the "long timeless journey" of her people, has transcended "every shade of persecution" and has attained an "all inclusive manner--wherein was drawn and mingled the pursued and the pursuer alike" (p. 72). Her musing capacity has given her "the unfathomable patience of a god in whom all is changed into wisdom, all experience and all life a handkerchief of wisdom when the grandiloquence of history and civilizations was past" (p. 72). Certainly the embroidered handkerchief is a fine image for the reflective musing of the creative mind--work done in the interstices of a bare grid of time and space, making new connections, revealing hidden patterns. Her musing was, says the narrator, "the subtlest labor and sweat of all time in the still music of the senses and of design" (p. 72).

Abandoning their social identities, the crew guided by the Arawak woman move into namelessness and silence, a via *negativa* that will bring them to self-knowledge. Names and words, they discover, are false, though necessary, constructions representing appearance but forever concealing even where they intend to reveal. Movement into silence brings the men to a different way of apprehending reality. Stripped of their capacity to name the world (a transaction that asserts the "I" at the expense of the named Other) they can only behold the world (assuming the role of womblike "eye" in which the Other is birthed). "Everyone paid silent tribute in the breakfastless early morning. None dared to say anything yet knowing their common speech was the debased coinage and currency of the dreaming folk. Silence seemed golden now and superior to the universal mask and ironic disavowal of principle in the nameless indestructible soul" (p. 93). Naming is evaluation with "debased currency" (p. 93)--a "distortion and debasement" of the Other. Silence, on the other hand, is "golden" (p. 93). Like the embroidery on the Arawak woman's kerchief, it is the plentitude within the womb of space that has been "named" absence by the crew's language. The crew speak a "hard and bitter style of words": (p. 43), and so do not understand the language of the folk--their "tricky" (trickster) speech (p. 43), which Donne disparagingly calls "blasted Buck talk" (p. 60).

Since the men do not understand her speech, the old woman points, and it is Vigilance, alert to her silent signifying, who first comes to his moment of vision outside the stream. Her pointing makes him aware of a "spidery skeleton . . . that danced and gambolled" (p. 103). It is Wishrop, resurrected after his death in the stream, and now climbing on "half-spidery feet" (p. 103) up the "vertical floor" of the cliff. Following her finger, Vigilance sees petroglyph ducks suddenly fly out of the stream, and mythic creatures (caught halfway in their metamorphosis), "half-donkey and half-cow . . . seething with fear as they plunged into the river" (p. 104). Everything the woman oints to confirms for Vigilance an ongoing creation that defies all images of stasis and death. Finally she points to "the blue ring of pentecostal fire in God's eye as it wheeled around him above the dreaming memory and prison of life until it melted where neither wound nor witch stood" (p. 116).

This last, to the material eye, was merely a parrot, but Vigilance has come to vision beyond the material as he ascends by "spidery misstep[s]" (p. 108) up the fragile "ladder" leading out of the stream. He achieves a momentary still point of spec-tatorial powers where his fragmented (framed) perception becomes a vision of undifferentiated wholeness. Here, the broken god is again renewed, made whole. Loss of familiar premises evokes an "intricate horror of space," but yields, paradoxically, a vision of order, as Vigilance sees "Winthrop's spider and transubstantiation: wheel and web, sunlight, starlight, all wishful substance violating and altering and annihilating shape and matter and invoking eternity only and space and musical filament and design" (p. 105). Life, he now perceives, is "a spider and wheel of baptism--infinite and expanding--on which he found himself pinned and bent" (p. 105).

Vigilance, in his own spider metamorphosis, becomes more like Anancy, an oracular muse. From his new perspective, the material is backgrounded--"the stream sang darkly"--and absent spaces are brought to the foreground: "and the stars and harmony of space turned into images of light" (p. 105). Broken god, on stilted "perch" and in oracular "cave," he is the trickster par excellence, renewing himself from within and so transcending death: "Millions of years had passed he knew until now he felt bruised and wounded beyond words and his limbs had crawled and still flew. He had slept in a cradle of branches and in a cave overlooking the chasm of time . . . . From his godlike perch he discerned the image of the musing boat in which they had come" (pp. 117-118). Anancy transforms himself into a musing subject. His endless signifying upon the structures of signification is akin to embroidery as he converts absence into presence, deprivation into plenitude.

Deprivation converted into plentitude through the inspiration of a folk muse is similarly the pattern in Carroll's story. Carroll, youngest member of the crew, is Schomburg's stepson. The boy's true paternity is not known, and Schomburg wishes to give his own name to his wife's child. But Carroll's mother refuses. This is how the incident is perceived through the eye of Vigilance, Schomburg's son:

Who and what was Carroll? Schomburg had glimpsed, Vigilance knew with an inborn genius and primitive eye, the living and the dead folk, the embodiment of hate and love, the ambiguity of everyone and no-one. He had recognized his true son, nameless out of shame and yet named with a new distant name by a muse and mother to make others equally nameless out of mythical shame and a name, and to forge for their descendants new mythical farflung relationships out of their nameless shame and fear. (p. 83)

Harris here reaches back to the naming of slaves, the adoption of the master's name, the loss of identity that accompanies such naming, and the permanent record and indictment of Europe that linger in the very names of people and landscape. But Carroll's naming says much more, invokes existential musing through the question, Who and what was Carroll?[28] "Carroll" is an androgynous marker. It also is music--an infinitely various blues song. Yet the naming of others is "a partial rehabilitation" of the namer's self, "a basking in ... the degradation and misery" of the Other (p. 100). It is thus the "darkest narcissism" in Schomburg that makes him fight against "accepting Carroll's name as Carroll, against relinquishing paternity to someone who was still untouched by and unknown to the spirit of guilt" (p. 83). Schomburg's impulse is to reduce Carroll to a unit of commercial exchange, rehabilitating himself by "basking in [his stepson's] degradation" (p. 100).

Only Carroll's "muse and mother" (significantly a feminine figure) dares to accept the namelessness and deprivation of his fatherless state and transform it into wholeness. She insists that the feminine alterity within the masculine not be stifled. In the final vision of the falls the narrator says, "One was what I am in the music--buoyed and supported above dreams by the undivided soul and anima in the universe" (p. 152). Carroll, refusing to be named anything other than the male plus female song he is, is the first to discover his step in the "dance of all fulfillment" that Donne comes to tread so slowly and painfully.

For Donne, the "only one in their midst who carried on his sleeve the affectation of a rich first name" (p. 84) is the antithesis of the nameless Carroll. Donne's spider metamorphosis as he climbs from the stream is a total paradigm shift in which the material constructs he had premised his life on suddenly appear as nothingness: "An abstraction grew around him ... nothing else ... the ruling abstraction of himself which he saw reflected nowhere. He was a ruler of men and a ruler of nothing. The sun rose into the blinding wall and river before him filling the stream and water with melted gold. He dipped his hand in but nothing was there" (pp. 128-129). Materially rich, Donne is unable to hold the true "gold" of El Dorado.

It is in the visions of the fall that Donne finally comes to see, that is, he becomes truly blind to his former perceptions. Appropriately, since the section is about the paradigm shift that makes new perceptions possible, there is abundant symbolic reference to frames. Three major visions occur: first, a carpenter working in a sealed room; second, a mother with her child; and third, a cosmic tree of life that is in perpetual metamorphosis. The entire passage culminates the novel's rich intertextuality with John Donne's "Hymne to God in His Sicknesse."

John Donne's poem, in which he anticipates his imminent death, is a threshold experience. He sees his body as a flat map --a perception he dismisses as illusory when he declared that in reality his "east" and "west" are but one point. The conceit goes further to declare that death and the resurrection are equally one point, and that "Christes crosse" (bespeaking death) and "Adams Tree" (restoration of the Tree of Life to redeemed humanity) "stood in one place." Donne denies images of sacrifice and insists that what appear to be "straits" of suffering are merely thresholds to a new world and new dimensions of life.

Harris's intertextuality takes the same conceit but gives new meanings to the boundary or threshold. As trickster-Anancy, he is concerned with the marketplace or cross(roads) with Europe-- that static polarized structuring that perpetually devalues and reifies the Caribbean folk. *Palace*, however, denies the validity of images of stasis and sacrifice and insists that out of the "death" of cultures in the Caribbean melting pot a new creativity is released. The novel replaces the fixity and stasis of the House structure with images of an ongoing creation, a never-ceasing metamorphosis. Thus the fixed and sacrificial "cross" of the crossroads is transformed into a redemptive threshold: Adam's ceaselessly growing Tree of Life.

A curious loss of boundaries occurs in the first vision of the carpenter. Donne, hammering on the windowpane, is unable to penetrate the room where the carpenter is at work, yet a swallow, framed in a picture on the wall within, "flew and dashed through the veil and window . . . flew in and out like a picture on the wall" (pp. 131-132). Donne, hammering away, has the fantasy experience that "it was he who stood within the room and the carpenter who stood reflected without" (p. 133). The carpenter, who is shaping his own body into a multifarious creation, "a divine alienation and translation of flesh and blood into everything and anything on earth" (p. 132), is also chiseling away at Donne, who feels himself "sliced with this skeleton saw by the craftsman of God in the windowpane of his eye" (p. 132). Described as an image of Death, the carpenter is, nevertheless, engaged in constant creation of living forms in his room, which is "old as a cave and as new as a study" (p. 133). Though the image is of a humble folk figure, there is immense wealth in the room: "The room grew crowded with visions he planed and chiseled and nailed into his mind, golden sights, the richest impressions of eternity. It was a millionaire's room--the carpenter's" (p. 134).

This threshold encounter at the "windowpane" of the perceiving eye, rich ás it is in paradox and ambiguity, appears to image the aesthetic experience. As Donne muses on the craftsman's work and the icons that fill the cave-womb in which the author's "most elaborate pictures and seasons [are] stored and framed and imagined" (p. 134), what he beholds is transformed even as he gazes. He discovers that *he* is the carpenter inside the room, and it is *his* flesh and blood that is being transubstantiated into new forms. Thus the wall between reader and text is abolished, and Donne the reader becomes Donne the writer-creator. The text that seemed to name and frame him into sacrificial scapegoat is transformed into a threshold where he now creatively names himself.

The masculine icon of the carpenter is complemented by a feminine icon of the mother and child framed "like an enormous picture" (p. 138). As Donne gazes at the second framed scene he at first sees nothing, but as he "reflects" and is "willing to be blinded" (p. 139)--that is, as he lays aside his habits of external analysis and measurement, he is drawn into vision. The poverty of the familiar icon--animal's trough, threadbare dress of the woman, helpless frailty of the fatherless child--is transformed into a vision of splendor, of the spirit of life eternally reincarnated in physical forms:

Not a grain of her dress but shone with her hair, clothing her threadbare limbs in the melting plaits of herself. Her ancient dress was her hair after all, falling to the ground and glistening and waving until it grew so frail and loose and endless, the straw in the cradle entered and joined it and the whole room was enveloped in it as a melting essence yields itself and spreads itself from the topmost pinnacle and star into the roots of self and space. (p. 139)

Creation again is presented as a dialogue between reader and text. The icon becomes rich at the moment when it is birthed again in the womb of Donne's musing eye.

The third vision (which occurs significantly on the seventh day of creation) is a vision of endless metamorphosis:

I saw the tree in the distance wave its arms and walk when I looked at it through the spiritual eye of the soul. First it shed its leaves sudden and swift as if the gust of the wind that blew had ripped it almost bare. The bark and wood turned to lightning flesh and the sun which had been suspended from its

head rippled and broke into stars that stood where the shattered leaves had been in the living wake of the storm. The
enormous starry dress it now wore spread itself all around into
a full majestic gown from which emerged the intimate column
of a musing neck, face and hands, and twinkling feet. The
stars became peacocks' eyes, and the great tree of flesh and
blood swirled into another stream that sparkled with divine
feathers where the neck and the hands and the feet had been
nailed. (p. 146)

This vision is the culmination of what has been portrayed in the
earlier icons. Repeatedly images of sacrifice--"shattered" leaves,
"ripped" bark and wood, "nailed" hands and feet--give way to new
creation, first tree, then flesh, then stars, then peacock. The
cosmic tree combines the carpenter (redemptive creator in
crucified victim) and the madonna (immaculate conception of the
Word in the womb of nature). It draws together images of
sacrifice and renewed life, masculinity and femininity, earth and
sky, animate and inanimate. The image not only defies all
boundaries of opposition and hierarchy, but combines in mutual
reflection the various mythologies of humanity: the crucifixion
of Christian myth, fugitive gods turned into constellations of
stars in Arawak creation myths, and the peacock's tail and cosmic
tree of alchemical lore.

The peacock itself becomes the "palace of the universe"--not
fixed House of institutionalized structure, but a place of living
dialogue where "the windows of the soul looked out and in" (p.
146). For Harris's vision is of a community of musing subjects
engaged in a sacramental mutual reflection and mutual re-creati-
on: "The living eyes in the crested head were free to observe the
twinkling stars and eyes and windows on the rest of the body and
the wings" (pp. 146-147).

In the context of literary criticism, such images as Harris uses
suggest that each text is rewritten as it is read creatively by each
new reader. Canonicity and a House of institutionalized art thus
become meaningless concepts, since the reader's creativity is now
the evaluative gauge.

The final climax of *Palace* echoes John Donne's words "I shall
be made thy musique." We hear Carroll's whistling, which, in
response to the constantly metamorphosing reality he beholds is,
itself, in constant metamorphosis: "It seemed to break and mend
itself always--tremulous, forlorn, distant, triumphant, the echo of
sound so pure and outlined in space it broke again into a mass of
music" (p. 147). The men--all so very different, all gazing from
their respective framed windows in the peacock's tail-- become
hollow womblike spaces in which a cosmic harmony can echo.
"One was what I am in the music," the narrator discovers: the
music is *one* and perfect, but each echoing mouth sings it

differently. The Word is forever reborn from the "immaculate conception" in the musing "eye."

When the reader is taken to be the locus of creative energy (not the authored text itself), a paradigm shift has occurred that has ramifications in the social context in which literature exists. Western individualism and authoritarianism, her hierarchies and identities are challenged by a carnivalesque upturning of the world characterized by pluralism, community, heterogeneity, and ongoing dialectic. The House of authority is found to be too limited to contain the ambiguities and paradoxes that a plural vision brings to light: "In my Father's house are many mansions."

Roland Barthes has complained that "our literature is characterized by the pitiless divorce which the literacy institution maintains between the producer of the text and its user, between its owner and its customer, between its author and its reader."[29] Barthes's response to this commercial negation of the reader's creativity is to assert the value not of the "readerly" but of the "writerly text."[30] For Barthes, the role of literature as work is "to make the reader no longer a consumer, but a producer of the text."[31] In fact, the writerly text as Barthes defines it is not a book, but "*ourselves writing*, before the infinite play of the world (the world as function) is traversed, intersected, stopped, plasticized, by some singular system (Ideology, Genus, Criticism) which reduces the plurality of entrances, the opening of networks, the infinity of languages."[32]

Palace of the Peacock both depicts its characters as writers and summons its readers to a "plurality of entrances, [an] opening of networks, [an] infinity of languages." The novel is, thus, a "writerly" work par excellence. Its characters, metamorphosed into Anancy spiders climbing out of the stream, are readers being transformed into writers, consumers into producers. They are people who, in rejecting the name given them in a text authored by another (as Carroll's musing mother refused the name of patriarchal authority for her son), move into an (androgynous) namelessness that is, in fact, not deprivation but an assertion of the infinite plurality of the self.

Notes

1. Helene Cixous, "Where Is She?" in *New French Feminisms: an Anthology*, ed. Elaine Marks and Isabelle de Courtivron (Amherst: University of Massachusetts Press, 1980), p. 97.

2. George Lamming, *The Pleasures of Exile* (London: Michael Joseph, 1960), pp. 109-110.

3. Annette Kolodny, *The Lay of the Land: Metaphor as Experience and History in American Life and Letters* (Chapel Hill: University of North Carolina Press, 1975), p. 88.

4. Ibid., p. 137.

5. Carolyn Merchant, *The Death of Nature* (New York: Harper and Row, 1980), p. 165.

6. Kolodny, *Land*, pp. 144-145.

7. Ibid., pp. 159-160.

8. Merchant, *Nature*, p. 295.

9. George Lamming, *Natives of My Person* (London: Longman, 1972), p. 13. All subsequent references will be to this edition.

10. The historical accuracy of Lamming's work can be seen by referring to a text such as Daniel P. Mannix and Malcolm Cowley, *Black Cargoes: A History of the Atlantic Slave Trade* (New York: Viking Press, 1972). The dissolute behavior of European sailors, their decimation by disease, the use by Columbus of bloodhounds to put down an Indian "uprising" in Haiti, the suicide of slaves, and the occasional case of insanity among both slaves and slavers--all are documented. But Lamming freely transgresses the boundaries between history and legend, introducing, for instance, the Indians' digging of graves for their European invaders. The factual, his technique implies, is not necessarily the true.

11. "During the time I was engaged in the slave trade I never had the least scruples as to its lawfulness" The Reverend John Newton, quoted by Mannix and Cowley, *Black Cargoes*, p. 131.

12. Martin Heidegger, *Poetry, Language, and Thought*, trans. Albert Hofstadter (New York: Harper, 1971), p. 47.

13. Lamming adds an "s" to his name. To avoid confusion, I adhere to Lamming's spelling throughout. Eden's account also mentions a disease that caused the crew to die off "sometimes four or five in a day" (p. 197).

14. Richard David, ed., *Hakluyt's Voyages* (Boston: Houghton Mifflin, 1981), p. 194.

15. Ibid., p. 194.

16. Ibid., p. 197.

17. Ibid., p. 197.

18. An image used frequently in *Season of Adventure*, as I have discussed in Chapter I.

19. Here the House/landscape duality is invoked with a definite privileging of the landscape.

20. I must mention, too, in this connection, Victor Questel's work on the Blues: "Blues in Caribbean Poetry," In Kairi '78: pp. 51-54, and "The Blue Note in Caribbean Poetry," in *Trinidad and Tobago Review 11* (1978): 5, 7, 10, and 31; and Maureen Warner Lewis's linguistic analysis "The African Impact on Language and Literature in the English-speaking Caribbean," in *Africa and the Caribbean: The Legacies of a Link*, Margaret Crahan and Franklin Knight (Baltimore: Johns Hopkins University Press, 1979).

21. Wilson Harris, *The Womb of Space* (Westport, Conn.: Greenwood Press, 1983), p. 120.

22. Ibid., p. 122.

23. Ibid., p. 127.

24. Ibid., p. 13.

25. In a lecture given at the University of Guyana in 1978, Harris said: "What one is searching for is community, and community means that one has to be able to live with many cultures, contrasting cultures, and realize that one's sovereign instruments are partial, and because one sees this, because one accepts one's limits, paradoxically one is open to a ceaseless creative task, because then you begin to bring together what appear to be wholly incompatible realms," Harris, "The Uses of Myth," unpublished lecture.

26. John Thieme, "The Legacy of Conquest," *Caribbean Contact* (March 1980), pp. 17-18.

27. Ibid., p. 18.

28. Lewis Carroll was, of course, the pseudonym of Charles Lutwidge Dodgson, whose fantasy *Alice through the Looking Glass*, like all of Harris's work, is an intriguing study of inverted images and reflections. The implicit suggestion here is that all names are false masks--pseudonyms.

29. Roland Barthes, *S/Z* (New York: Hill and Wang, 1974), p. 4.

30. Ibid., p. 4.

31. Ibid., p. 5.

32. Ibid., p. 6.

Conclusion

New and old
is the face of the world's great grief,
a kind of music we listen to and hear
when the toil of silence builds
our house of language in this wind's
throat, the grim larynx.

Martin Carter[1]

An approach to the works of Lamming and Harris such as I have demonstrated in the three preceding essays decodes the Caribbean text in exciting and illuminating ways. What began as an exploratory probing of boundaries has led to a discussion that embraces, among other things, the role of the artist in a Third World society, the phenomenon of mental colonization, "reading" as metaphor for perception, and a Lacanian model of desire confined by the structures of language.

Viewed from the margins, each of the six novels can be read as a rite of passage leading out of a "colonized" landscape of binary oppositions, through a disorienting limbo or middle passage, and into new modes of perception where relationships, dialogue, and pluralism replace apparently irreconcilable polarizations, and an ongoing revision of premises is posited as the fundamental prerequisite for an authentic relationship with reality. Whereas European imperialism established a macabre rite of passage into a colonized world, Lamming and Harris identify the need to reverse that journey, going back into the womb, as it were, to be reborn to a new world vision.

In this new rite of passage, undergone by protagonist and eader alike, the artist functions as shaman. Indeed, both Lamm-

ing and Harris are profoundly and explicitly concerned in their
novels with the role of the artist in effecting social change, and
artist figures appear in all six texts under consideration. Chiki
with his fictions and paintings, G with his diary, and the
Commandant's wife with her "leaves" are all artist figures
interacting with an oppressive written text, as are Cristo with his
fictions and the carnival revelers he meets, Donne with his craft
and the signifying lost tribe, Frank Wellington with his marginalia, and Hope in his masquerade glory. In each case, suppressed creativity is revealed to be an energy that threatens
structure--desire bursting the confines of the containing word.

"Reading," says Terry Eagleton, "is an ideological decipherment of an ideological product."[2] Decipherment of a received
structure takes a variety of forms in the novels discussed. The
reader is required to abandon conventional modes of reading and
engage in a new approach. Harris's work resists every attempt to
read it as one reads traditional novels, demanding, rather, a
totally new response to character, chronology, plot, and metaphor.
Lamming's work, though less radically innovative in technique,
yields far more to the reader who backgrounds conventions of
plot and character development and pays attention to the
deconstructive activity at work within the text.

Certainly both writers highlight language and technique as
self-conscious subject matter and so focus on the crucial role of
language as medium of exchange in the colonization process. A
colonized world, people, psyche--even landscape--is a function of
the controlling Word: hegemony finds its ultimate strength in
language. Speaking of Pa in *Castle*, Sandra Paquet writes, "The
transformation of language which occurs in Pa's attempt to
articulate a vision that transcends the mental and physical
limitations of slavery and colonization reflects Lamming's own
efforts to free the language from its historical role as a major
colonizing agent."[3] In similar vein, Sandra Drake says, "Harris's
art reveals his faith in the resources of language both to express
and to create an understanding that will constitute . . . a 'new
architecture of the world',"[4] and again, "Harris's use of language
undermines it as supportive of empire."[5]

Empire building is characterized by the setting of boundaries,
and boundaries express the principle of ownership--of lands, of
people, of culture. But it is at the level of *language* that such
proprietorship is most fundamentally asserted, and this occurs in
two distinct ways. First, the colonizer imposes his own language
(French, Spanish, English) on the territory he claims, and so
ensures that the very mode of communication is always encoded
with his worldview. Secondly as a man of the book, the colonizer
introduces a cultural polarization that names the written superior
to the oral, and by ignoring the oral, apparently reduces it to
silence.

Walter Ong has explored the fundamental shift that occurs
when writing takes the place of orality. In putting knowledge
into writing, Ong argues, we separate it from consciousness,
making it a thing that can be "'parked' outside consciousness."[6]
Knowledge thus reified, one could infer, can be owned and
marketed in a way that oral utterance cannot be. But Ong goes
further to point out that "many if not most persons in technological cultures are strongly conditioned to think unreflectively that
the printed word is the real word, and that the spoken word is
inconsequential."[7]   In oral cultures, though, knowledge is ex-
periential, and certainly cannot be owned; it cannot even be
conceived of as a self-contained system outside of lived experience. Clearly the interface between oral and written reveals
totally different modes of apprehending reality. One can infer
from Ong's discussion that Western concepts of authorship,
copyright, and a "body of knowledge" marketable by way of a
"formal education system" are arbitrary formulations that are
immediately called into question when set beside a radically oral
perception in which the word is continuous with lived experience, and knowledge is intuited. The difference, says Ong,
is "between total immersion and objective understanding."[8]
     It follows that when Harris and Lamming set a radically oral
culture over against a culture dominated by the written word
(Bible, great tradition, history, law), they are operating within a
liminal space that exposes the assumptions and arbitrary hierarchies of the "house of language" and reveals the values of a
silenced culture assumed by technological man to be "inconsequential." Their assault on the word by which an imperialist
worldview is expressed thus erodes the very premises that
authorize colonizing activities. Their novels play in the margins
of the written and give voice to the silenced oral, parodically
undercutting all the assumptions of technological culture.
     Reference to Roland Barthes's readerly-writerly continuum is
pertinent here. In *S/Z* Barthes writes:

A multivalent text can carry out its basic duplicity only if it
subverts the opposition between true and false, if it fails to
attribute quotations (even when seeking to discredit them) to
explicit authorities, if it flouts all respect for origin, paternity,
propriety, if it destroys the voice which could give the text its
("organic") unity, in short, if it coldly and fraudulently
abolishes quotation marks, which must, as we say, in all
honesty, enclose a quotation and juridically distribute the
ownership of the sentences to their respective proprietors, like
the subdivisions of a field. For multivalence (contradicted by
irony) is a transgression of ownership.[9]

In their "transgression of ownership" of the final word of

authority, then, and in their subversion of the opposition between
true and false, Harris and Lamming are engaging in revolutionary activity, and their insistence (more emphatically displayed in
Harris, it is true) that the reader becomes writer, the consumer
becomes producer of the work, is a literary strategy totally
hostile to authoritarian ideologies. As I have indicated, to reject
the premise of ownership, as both Lamming and Harris do, is to
dislodge the cornerstone of the entire colonizing venture.

Both Lamming and Harris focus on the very process of
reading, showing it to be an arbitrary and ideological framing of
the text. The reader follows the protagonist as she/he moves
from one reading of reality to another, and, in so doing, becomes
conscious of ideological frame-ups. This self-consciousness about
perception is still further heightened in other techniques. Both
writers substitute for the conventional epic protagonist a
plurality of perspectives in dialogue, and imply in their characterization technique that no individual can function as sole
authority. In requiring the reader to be cowriter, unraveling the
conflicting views presented, they assert further that they
themselves are merely writers, not authorities.   Such carnivalesque techniques invite an ongoing revision of premises and
abandoning of preconceptions, so that dialogic structure in the
novel becomes, in fact, revolutionary statement. The open text
is an ironic commentary on all closed systems.

Another linguistic strategy is the ubiquitous use of punning to
lay bare the opacity of words and so erode their authority as
fixed and final "naming" agents. The novels of both of these
writers enter a liminal space between the written texts of Western
culture and a non-Western oral tradition. Religious, literary, and
historical texts are all subjected to ironic examination. Biblical
allusions and references to Christian practices and sacraments are
inserted not to affirm a Christian orthodoxy, but parodically--the
implication being that there is always an alternative reading of
the signs. Thus Lamming introduces his "born again" motif in
Castle, the horrific sacrament of black flesh in *Natives*, and the
baptism of "foolish Virgin(ian)s" in Mary-land in *Season*. Harris,
similarly, names his Cristo, Magda, Sharon, and Abram in *The
Whole Armour* (whose very title is taken from Paul's letter to the
Ephesians 6:11), yet brings the Christian text into dialogue with
Taoism, alchemy, folk legend and so on.

In addition to confronting a religious text, both also enter a
liminal space between the Western literary tradition and an oral
folk culture. Lamming's fascination with Shakespeare's *Tempest*
as outlined in *Pleasures of Exile* is well known.   Prospero,
Caliban, Miranda and the sea change overtly permeate his novels
Of Age and Innocence and *Water with Berries*, and the theme of
language (Prospero's "gift" to Caliban) is ever present in *Castle*
and *Season*, while *Natives* is a recapitulation of all those many

journeys made by Prospero to Caliban's island. Similarly Harris's intertextuality with a written culture is ubiquitous. Yeats, Eliot, Heidegger, Bachelard, Blake, Donne and scores of other poets and philosophers are invoked. Indeed, a search for sources in Harris's work is more than daunting, though Caribbean critic Michael Gilkes has traced an abundance of them.[10] But although Harris employs abundant literary allusions, he is by no means imitating or invoking authorities. To speak of his "indebtedness" to Blake, Eliot, Yeats is to miss the point entirely! Like the *houngan*'s tent in *Season*, where canonized Christian saints engage in conversation with African deities, the novels of both Harris and Lamming occupy a dangerous-sacred liminal ground where canonical texts of the great tradition undergo deconstruction as they are juxtaposed with non-Western orality--petroglyph and calypso, Amerindian legend and Anancy story, rites for the spirits of forest and river, and signifying events such as masquerade dance and steel band.

As with biblical and literary texts, so with history. Both Lamming and Harris interact with actual events of the distant and more recent past. It is possible to trace in both writers allusions to the trek from Siberia, voyages of conquest, the middle passage from West Africa, emancipation, indentureship and independence, and the several waves of exodus--to Panama, to Britain, to North America. Recent political events appear, such as the Burnham-Jagan rivalry and the movement toward totalitarian control in Guyana, as well as the "flight of the landlord," post Independence neocolonialism in Barbados, and the region's aborted attempt at federation. Further, because both writers are still living, and because of the parochial nature of Caribbean society, it is tempting to engage in an archaeology of the novels, establishing links between literary work and historical event--even to identify people and places mentioned in the fiction.

But such traditional scholarly methods of empirical background research are perhaps invalidated by the technique of these two writers, for Harris and Lamming are not writing history but creating myths. Indeed they question the very notion of history as information contained in a written text. Their concern is with rereading the historical text to discover the intrahistorical. "Rereading," says Barthes, "draws the text out of its internal chronology ('this happens *before* or *after* that') and recaptures a mythic time (without *before* or *after*)."[11]

Critic Selwyn Cudjoe recognizes such a mythic impulse in Harris's fiction but celebrates Lamming rather for his "socio-psychological realism." Harris's "magical realism," Cudjoe claims, "restates historical experience in archetypal terms with a mythology and cosmology particularly Caribbean."[12] Lamming, in contrast, he sees as being able "to elucidate the casual relationship between the opposing tendencies in Caribbean society."[13] Because of this frame of social realism, Cudjoe can write at length on Lamming, but only briefly on Harris. Yet Lamming, too, despite his incorporation of traceable historical event, is very much a mythmaker. Moreover, his skepticism about history as a valid system of knowing one's past or as being helpful in living one's present is felt pervasively in his fiction. The historical method of academic research into Lamming's novels is consequently of dubious value since it marginalizes the literariness wherein lies their revolutionary statement.

There exists, even as clearly as *Castle*, both a chronological forward movement, and a reflective revision of that progression through time, and this principle of the "backward glance" becomes increasingly prominent as the mythopoetic takes the place of realism in Lamming's later works. In *Natives of My Person* the writer produces a deliberate blurring of temporal boundaries, with the result that the voyage to Black Rock contains all West Indian history from Columbus to the present and presents colonialism on a wider, metaphorical scale that embraces racism, sexism, class conflict, and destruction of the ecosystem. It is, I suggest, not so much social or psychological realism that gives Lamming's fiction its power; rather it is the mythic energy. His repeated rites of passage between a capitalist, technological culture and a traditional folk culture transform the House-plantation landscape of a polarized world into a metaphor for the entire system of Western domination, and the silenced Folk becomes a metaphor for values and modes of being-in-the-world that are left out of consideration by that Western capitalist-technological patriarchal model.

Lamming's mythicizing of the colonial experience is revealed more vividly when, in addition to anthropological insights, a feminist perspective is brought to his novels. Where the anthropological Anancy reading reveals a pervasive threat of castration and a perennial reassembling of the god's "parts," an explicitly feminist reading reveals an intense power struggle that polarizes the world into dominant (male) and dominated (female). Whereas castration images link with exploited groups of men (Sasha in *Natives*, for instance, is used and dressed as a girl), exploited groups of women are associated with silence, madness, self-mutilation and eventual aggressive destruction of the male. Virgin lands become a vagina dentata, and the womb becomes a tomb as female nature rises to destroy technological man with his ships and weapons, his charts of ownership and his written word of authority. The metamorphosis of history into myth is complete.

Harris's rejection of history as linear sequence of events has still more far-reaching effects on his fiction. Indeed, Harris's technique at every point refutes the fact-oriented certainties on which a historical method thrives. His characters drift in and out of each other, time sequence is carefully established and subsequently abandoned, plot line is minimal, and events presented as fact early in a novel are later exposed as fictions or misconceptions. Location is unclear, and history is deliberately mixed with patent fantasy. A blurring of the fact-fiction boundary is found everywhere. As Sandra Drake says, "Harris establishes the plots in these novels only to undercut them, thereby making an implicit critique of the 'series of adventures,' in Harris's words, which he thinks present a misleading and dangerous way of conceptualizing history."[14]

Embedded in the narrative structures employed by Lamming and Harris, then, is a total rejection of the very concept of history. Written historical texts lift events out of time and fix them in space so that they become solid objects--an architecture of a people's past acts. No such architecture exists in oral culture, where memory and imagination make oral recapitulation of the past a renewed, corporate immersion into relived experience. In their fiction, Lamming and Harris do not merely name an alternative historical record--a reconstruction of acts of the colonized. Rather, they demystify history, exposing institutionalized history writing as an entirely arbitrary systematizing of selected events (akin to fictive narrative) that serves an ideological purpose but is never, nor ever can be objectively factual. Terry Eagleton was referring to the literary text when he wrote, "There can be contradiction only between ideology and what it occludes--history itself,"[15] but the principle applies to the writing of history itself. Indeed, Harris makes the same point when his character Hope, at the end of *Genesis of the Clowns*, emigrates into "the *telling* silences secreted in the family of the Word" (p. 148, italics mine).

One final aspect of boundaries and perception remains for consideration: the sociogeographical landscape that shaped the developing consciousness of Lamming and Harris respectively. Harris brings to his fiction a mental landscape profoundly influenced by the landscape of his homeland--a land where interfaces are multiple, and where the very physical geography denies rigid boundaries; rivers erode banks, rains flood the city, bush quickly obscures roads and landmarks, while insect life together with weathering maintains a perpetual assault on monumental structures of every kind.

Lamming's, in contrast, is essentially a black-white world: Big England-Little England, tourist-native, rich-poor, consumer-producer, capital-labor, work-play. Above all there is the land--and the sea. No hinterland; no ties except an umbilical cord reaching across the Atlantic either to Mother England, or, alternatively, to Mother Africa. In Guyana, French, Dutch, and British were colonial powers at various times, and even Spanish settlements can be found. Barbados, in contrast, was occupied only by the British. Guyana still has an Amerindian community pursuing a more or less traditional life-style, but Barbados has no indigenous people left.[16] The racial mixture in Guyana includes the indigenous Amerindians, Indians, and Madeiran Portuguese (whose forbears came as indentured laborers following emancipation); Chinese (both those who came during the period of indentureship and hundreds who have immigrated during the past three decades; the Creole community (descendants of white landowners); and the descendants of Africans who came as slaves from West Africa. Barbados has no such cosmopolitan flavor. With the exception of a small Syrian-Asian community, her people fall into two groups--descendants of Europeans and descendants of Africans, with in-between shades of brown resulting from miscegenation. Where Barbados is cut off by the sea from non-English speakers and other cultures, Guyana borders on Venezuela, Suriname, and Brazil, so that an Incan-Mayan connection is more logically valid than a European one. The plurality of religious and customs in Guyana engages her peoples in an ongoing "cultural collision," to use Harris's words, whereas in the basic dualism of Barbadian society the sole challenge to Christianity is found in surviving African religious forms. A vibrant tourist industry constantly reconfirms Barbadian links with Europe and North America, while Guyana remains virtually free of such influence. Finally, the very size of Guyana (and the inaccessibility of many hinterland areas) ensures a heterogeneity of culture such as would be impossible in the very small island of Barbados.

Shaped by his island experience, Lamming urges a "sea change" but finds that he has merely inverted the model, not changed it. Black replaces white, and federal building replaces the landlord's House on the hill, but to the end Mrs. Gore-Britain remains the landlady who has to be destroyed--the House still has to be burned down. Harris, in contrast, proposes a rite of passage into perceptual regions beyond the false dualities. Turning his back on the northern connection, he reaches into the Heartland, where he finds links with Arawak and Indian, African and Chinese, Mayan and Incan. By positing a dialectical model, he asserts that science and art, silence and the word, wealth and poverty, male and female, technology and nature--all our unreal binary oppositions--are, in fact, latent within each other. Thus, where Lamming opposes only African and European deities in the *houngan*'s tents, Harris assembles all humanity's sacra, insisting that we find ways to speak to each other between our perceptual metaphors in a limbo space freed from authoritarian stances of domination.

"Interfacing" has become a well-worked word in the past decade. Closed-system paradigms have been rejected in one academic discipline after another. In the late nineteenth century,

Darwin stressed the interrelatedness of animal life and the environment, while in the early twentieth, quantum theory and relativity theory made physical scientists more aware of the viewer's frame. In philosophy, Sartre and Heidegger have both argued that human beings grow through interaction with others, and increasingly the concept of subject area is being eroded as minds explore fertile interdisciplinary margins.

But while such interplay at the margins has become popular and fruitful in academia, it is still to be achieved in society. Imperial habits of perception persist, and a House-plantation frame-up continues to inform First-Third World economic domination, race- or gender-based ideologies, class attitudes, religious intolerance, and technological man's assumption that he owns and may freely exploit the earth. Because of our false premises of ownership and domination, we continue on our destructive course. Until we find a way to step out of the metaphor of commodification and ownership and relate within a complex network (web?) of open systems, imposing House and exploited plantation will remain. And while they do, so will Anancy, spinner of webs:

> the god stares down
> black beating heart of him breathing
> breathing
> consuming our wood
> and the words of our houses
> black iron-eye'd eater, the many eyed maker,
> creator, dry stony world-maker, word-breaker,
> creator . . .[17]

NOTES

1. Martin Carter, "As New and as Old," in *Poems of Affinity* (Georgetown, Guyana: Release Publications, 1980).

2. Terry Eagleton, *Criticism and Ideology* (London: Verse Editions, 1978), p. 62.

3. Sandra Pouchet-Paquet, *The Novels of George Lamming* (Kingston: Heinemann Educational Books, 1982), p. 7.

4. Sandra Drake, *Wilson Harris and the Modern Tradition* (Westport, Conn.: Greenwood Press, 1986), p. 185.

5. Ibid., p. 178.

6. Walter Ong, *Interfaces of the Word* (Ithaca, N.Y.: Cornell University Press, 1977), p. 297.

7. Ibid., p. 21.

8. Ibid., p. 290.

9. Roland Barthes, *S/Z* (New York: Hill and Wang, 1974), pp. 44-45).

10. Michael Gilkes, *Wilson Harris and the Caribbean Novel* (London: Longman, 1975).

11. Barthes, S/Z, p. 16.

12. Selwyn Cudjoe, *Resistance and Caribbean Literature* (Athens: Ohio University Press, 1980), p. 257.

13. Ibid., p. 272.

14. Drake, *Harris*, p. 5.

15. Eagleton, *Criticism and Ideology*, p. 95.

16. There are nine Amerindian tribes in Guyana: Akawaio, Arekuna, Arawak, Makushi, Patamuna, Wapishana, Warau, Carib, Wai-Wai.

17. E. K. Brathwaite, "Ananse," *Islands* (London: Oxford University Press, 1969), p. 6.

Bibliography

Babcock-Abrahams, Barbara, ed. *The Reversible World: Symbolic Inversion in Art and Society.* Ithaca: Cornell University Press, 1978.

_____. "'A Tolerated Margin of Mess': The Trickster and His Tales Reconsidered." *Journal of the Folklore Institute* 11 (1975): 147-186.

Bachelard, Gaston. *The Poetics of Space.* Translated by Maria Jolas. Toronto: Beacon Press, 1969.

Baker, Houston A., Jr. *Blues, Ideology, and Afro-American Literature: A Vernacular Theory.* Chicago: University of Chicago Press, 1984.

_____. *The Journey Back: Issues in Black Literature and Criticism.* Chicago: University of Chicago Press, 1980.

_____. "To Move without Moving: An Analysis of Creativity and Commerce in Ralph Ellison's Trueblood Episode." *P.M.L.A.* 98 (October 1983): 828-845.

Bakhtin, Mikhail. *Problems of Dostoevsky's Poetics.* Translated by R. W. Rotsel. Ann Arbor: Ardis, 1973.

Barthes, Roland. "Myth Today." In his *Mythologies.* Translated by Annette Lavers. New York: Hill and Wang, 1972.

_____. *S/Z.* New York: Hill and Wang, 1974.

Baugh, Edward. *Critics on Caribbean Literature.* New York: Allen and Unwin, 1978.

Bennett, Tony. *Formalism and Marxism.* London: Methuen and Co., 1979.

Bloom, Harold. *The Anxiety of Influence.* New York: Oxford University Press, 1973.

Brathwaite, Edward Kamau. "The African Presence in Caribbean Literature." *Daedelus* 103 (Spring, 1974): 73-109.

_____. "Houses in the West Indian Novel." *Literary Half-Yearly* 17 (1976): 111-121.

_____. "The Love Axe(1): Developing a Caribbean Aesthetic 1962-1974." In *Reading Black*, edited by Houston Baker, Jr., 20-36. Philadelphia: University of Pennsylvania, 1976.

_____. *Rights of Passage*. London: Oxford University Press, 1967.

Brown, Lloyd W. "West Indian Literature, Road to a 'New World' Sensibility." *Journal of Black Studies* 7: 411-436.

Buber, Martin. *I and Thou*. New York: Charles Scribner's Sons, 1958.

Burckhardt, Titus. *Alchemy*. Translated by William Stoddart. Baltimore: Penguin Books, 1971.

Carew, Jan. "The Caribbean Writer and Exile." *Caribbean Studies* 19 (April-July 1979): 111-132.

Carrington, John F. "The Talking Drums of Africa." *Scientific American* (December 1971): 90-94.

Chevalier, Jean, and Alain Gheerbrant, eds. *Dictionnaire des Symboles*. Paris: Seghers, 1969.

Cixous, Helene. "Where is She?" in *New French Feminisms: An Anthology*, ed. Elaine Marks and Isabelle de Courtivron. Amherst: University of Massachusetts Press, 1980.

Collier, Gordon. "Artistic Autonomy and Cultural Allegiance." *Literary Half-Yearly* 20: 93-105.

Coombs, Orde. *Is Massa Day Dead?* New York: Anchor, Doubleday, 1974.

Cox, Harvey. *The Feast of Fools*. Cambridge, Mass.: Harvard University Press, 1969.

Crahan, Margaret, and Franklin Knight. *Africa and the Caribbean: The Legacies of a Link*. Baltimore: Johns Hopkins University Press, 1979.

Daly, Mary. *Gyn/ecology: The Metaethics of Radical Feminism*. Boston: Beacon Press, 1978.

David, Richard, ed. *Hakluyt's Voyages*. Boston: Houghton Mifflin, 1981.

Derrida, Jacques. "Signature, Event, Context." *Glyph* 1, 172-197. Baltimore: Johns Hopkins University Press, 1976.

_____. *Speech and Phenomena*. Translated by David B. Allison. Evanston: Northwestern University Press, 1973.

_____. "Structure, Sign, and Play in the Discourse of the Human Sciences." In *Of Grammatology*, translated by Gayatri Spivak, 278-293. Baltimore: Johns Hopkins University Press, 1976.

Douglas, Mary. *Purity and Danger*. London: Routledge and Kegan Paul, 1966.

Drake, Sandra. *Wilson Harris and the Modern Tradition*. Westport, Conn.: Greenwood Press, 1986.

Eagleton, Terry. *Criticism and Ideology*. London: Verse Editions, 1978.

Ehrenzweig, Anton. *The Hidden Order of Art.* Berkeley: University of California Press, 1969.

Eliade, Mircea. *Myth and Reality.* New York: Harper and Row, 1963.

Eliot, T. S. "Tradition and the Individual Talent." In *The Sacred Wood.* London: Methuen and Co., 1969.

Ellison, Ralph. "Change the Joke and Slip the Yoke." *Shadow and Act* 45-59. New York: Random House, 1964.

Fanon, Frantz. *Black Skin, White Masks.* Translated by Charles Lam Markmann. New York: Grove Press, 1967.

_____. *The Wretched of the Earth.* Translated by Constance Farrington. New York: Grove Press, 1963.

Fiedler, Leslie A., and Houston A. Baker, Jr., eds. *English Literature: Opening up the Canon.* Baltimore: Johns Hopkins University Press, 1981.

Finnegan, Ruth. *Oral Literature in Africa.* Nairobi: Oxford University Press, 1976.

Fisher, Dexter, and Robert Stepto. *Afro-American Literature. The Reconstruction of Instruction.* New York: Modern Languages Association, 1979.

Freud, Sigmund. *The Interpretation of Dreams.* Translated by James Strachey. New York: Basic Books. 1955.

_____. *Totem and Taboo.* New York: Norton, 1952.

Gates, Henry Louis, Jr. "The 'Blackness of Blackness': A Critique of the Sign and the Signifying Monkey." *Critical Inquiry* 9 (June 1983): 685-723.

Geertz, Clifford. "Deep Play: Notes on the Balinese Cockfight." In his *Interpretation of Cultures*, 412-453. New York: Basic Books, 1973.

Gilbert, Sandra and Susan Gubar. *The Madwoman in the Attic.* New Haven: Yale University Press, 1979.

Gilkes, Michael. *The West Indian Novel.* Boston: G. K. Hall, 1981.

_____. *Wilson Harris and the Caribbean Novel.* London: Longman, 1975.

Goveia, Elsa. *A Study of the Historiography of the British West Indies.* Mexico, D.F., 1956.

Griffin, Susan. *Woman and Nature: The Roaring Inside Her.* New York: Harper and Row, 1978.

Griffiths, Gareth. *A Double Exile.* London: Marion Boyars, 1978.

Harris, Wilson. "Aspects of the Exploration of History." Unpublished lecture. University of Guyana, March 1978.

_____. *Genesis of the Clowns.* London: Faber and Faber, 1977.

_____. "History, Fable, and Myth in the Caribbean and the Guianas." In *Anagogic Qualities of Literature*, 120-131. Edited by Joseph P. Strelka. University Park and London: Pennsylvania State University Press, 1971.

_____. "Interior of the Novel: Amerindian/European/African Relations." In *National Identity: Papers Delivered at the*

Commonwealth Literature Conference, University of Queens-land. Brisbane August 9-15 1968, 138-147. Edited by K. L. Goodwin. London: Heinemann Press, 1970.

_____. _Palace of the Peacock._ London: Faber and Faber, 1960.

_____. "The Phenomenal Legacy." _Literary Half-Yearly_ 11 (July 1970): 1-6.

_____. _Tradition, the Writer, and Society._ London: New Beacon Publications, 1967.

_____. "The Uses of Myth." Unpublished lecture. University of Guyana, 1978.

_____. _The Whole Armour._ London: Faber and Faber, 1962; reprint, London: Faber and Faber, 1973.

_____. _The Womb of Space._ Westport, Conn: Greenwood Press, 1983.

Heidegger, Martin. _Poetry, Language, and Thought._ Translated by Albert Hofstadter. New York: Harper, 1971.

Hill, Errol. _The Trinidad Carnival: Mandate for a National Theatre._ Austin: University of Texas, 1972.

Jung, Gustav. _The Archetypes and the Collective Unconscious._ Translated by R. F. C. Hull. Princeton: Princeton University Press, 1968.

_____. _Mysterium Coniunctionis: Inquiry into the Separation and Synthesis of Psychic Opposites in Alchemy._ Translated by R. F. C. Hull. Princeton: Princeton University Press, 1970.

Kolodny, Annette. _The Lay of the Land: Metaphor as Experience and History in American Life and Letters._ Chapel Hill: University of North Carolina Press, 1975.

Lamming, George. _In the Castle of My Skin._ London: Longman, 1970.

_____. _Natives of My Person._ London: Longman, 1972.

_____. _The Pleasures of Exile._ London: Michael Joseph, 1960.

_____. _Season of Adventure._ London: Allison and Busby, 1979.

Lawrence, Leota. "From Cultural Ambivalence to the Celebration of the African Heritage in British West Indian Literature." _College Language Association Journal_ 23 (1979): 220-233.

Levi-Strauss, Claude. _Tristes Tropiques._ New York: Atheneum, 1964.

Maes, Jelinek, Hena. "The Myth of El Dorado in the Caribbean Novel." _Journal of Commonwealth Literature_ 6 (June 1971): 113-127.

_____. _Wilson Harris._ Boston: G. K. Hall, 1982. Makarius, Laura. "Ritual Clowns and Symbolic Behavior." _Diogenes_ 69 (1970): 44-73.

Mannix, Daniel P., and Malcolm Cowley. _Black Cargoes: A History of The Atlantic Slave Trade._ New York: Viking Press, 1972.

Marks, Elaine and Isabelle de Courtivron, eds. _New French Feminisms: An Anthology._ Amherst, Mass.: University of Massachusetts Press, 1980.

Mbiti, John S. *African Religions and Philosophy*. New York: Doubleday, 1970.

Merchant, Carolyn. *The Death of Nature*. New York: Harper and Row, 1980.

Munro, Ian, and Reinhard Sander. *Kas-Kas: Interviews with Three Caribbean Writers in Texas*. Austin: University of Texas Press, 1972.

Naipaul, V. S. *The Middle Passage*. London: Andre Deutsch, 1962.

Ngugi, Wa Thiong'o. *Homecoming: Essays on African and Caribbean Literature, Culture, and Politics*. London: Heinemann Educational Books, 1972.

Nietzsche, Friedrich. *The Birth of Tragedy*. Translated by Walter Kaufmann. New York: Vintage, 1967.

_____. *The Use and Abuse of History*. Translated by Adrian Collins. New York: Liberal Arts Press, 1957.

Ong, Walter. *Interfaces of the Word*. Ithaca, N.Y.: Cornell University Press, 1977.

_____. *The Presence of the Word*. New Haven: Yale University Press, 1967.

Ortega y Gasset, Jose. *The Modern Theme*. New York: Norton, 1933.

Peckham, Morse. *Man's Rage for Chaos*. New York: Schocken Books, 1967.

Pelton, Robert D. *The Trickster in West Africa: A Study of Mythic Irony and Sacred Delight*. Berkeley: University of California Press, 1980.

Piaget, Jean. *The Child and Reality*. New York: Grossman Publishers, 1973.

Pouchet-Paquet, Sandra. *The Novels of George Lamming*. Kingston: Heinemann Educational Books, 1982.

Radin, Paul. *The Trickster: A Study in American Indian Mythology*. New York: Greenwood Press, 1956.

Ramchand, Kenneth. "The Significance of the Aborigine in Wilson Harris's Fiction." *Literary Half-Yearly* 11 (1970): 7-16.

_____. *The West Indian Novel and Its Background*. New York: Barnes and Noble, 1970.

Rohlehr, Gordon. "The Creative Writer and West Indian Society." Kaie 11 (August 1973): 48-77.

_____. "The Folk in Caribbean Literature." *Tapia* 11 (December 1972): 7-8, 13-15.

_____. "Some Problems of Assessment." *Caribbean Quarterly* 17 (1971): 92-113.

Smith, Roland, ed. *Exile and Tradition. Studies in African and Caribbean Literature*. Halifax, Nova Scotia: 1976.

Thieme, John. "The Legacy of Conquest--An Interview with Wilson Harris." *Caribbean Contact* (March 1980): 17-18.

Turner, Victor. *Dramas, Fields, and Metaphors*. Ithaca, N.Y.:

Cornell University Press, 1974.

_____. *The Forest of Symbols*. Ithaca, N.Y.: Cornell University Press, 1967.

_____. "Myth and Symbol." In *International Encyclopedia of the Social Sciences*. New York: Macmillan, 1968.

_____. *The Ritual Process*. Chicago: Aldine Publishing, 1969. Van Gennep, Arnold. *The Rites of Passage*. Translated by Monika B. Vizedom. Chicago: University of Chicago Press, 1960.

Walcott, Derek. "The Caribbean--Culture or Mimicry?" *Journal of Interamerican Studies*. 16 (February, 1974): 3-13.

_____. "What the Twilight Says: An Overture." In *Dream on Monkey Mountain*. New York: Farrar, Straus, and Giroux, 1970.

Warner, Keith Q. *Kaiso! The Trinidad Calypso*. Washington: Three Continents Press, 1982.

Welsford, Enid. *The Fool: His Social and Literary History*. Gloucester, Mass.: Faber and Faber, 1935. Reprinted, 1966.

Wescott, Joan. "The Sculpture and Myths of Eshu-Elegba, the Yoruba Trickster." *Africa* 32 (October 1962): 336-353.

White, Hayden. *Tropics of Discourse*. Baltimore: Johns Hopkins University Press, 1978.

Wynter, Sylvia. "Jonkonnu in Jamaica." *Jamaica Journal* 4 (June, 1970): 34-48.

_____. "Reflections on West Indian Writing and Criticism." *Jamaica Journal* 2 (December 1968): 24-32.

Index

Abraham, 35-36

Ambivalence, 10, 30; embrace of, 74; toward the land, 92; of man to woman, 36-37; prevalence of, 44; and signature, 83; in the *tonelle*, 20

Anancy, 2; artist as, 71-72; and creative disorder, 12, 41, 51; dialectic of, 52; as god of creation, 39, 52; and the marketplace, 11; as trader, 52. *See also* Trickster

Anthropological orientation, 9-11

Ariadne, 53

Art: creative disorder of, 9, 44; of the dispossessed, 72; and politics, 76

Artist: as Anancy, 71-72; as edgeman, 8; as expiatory figure of the tribe, 29-30; as novelist, 111; in the plantation model, 50; as shaman, 129-130; in society, 58; spider-creator as icon for, 2; tragedy of, 29; as trickster, 11

Babcock, Barbara, 51

Backward speech, 56

Barthes, Roland, 31, 125, 131, 133

Black and white imagery, 15-16

Black people: as composite scapegoat, 32-33; ultimate ambiguity of, 10

Blood imagery, 16

Bloom, Harold, 44

Boundaries, 14; collapse of, 74; danger in, 16; destruction of, 26; and empire building, 130; forces threatening, 30-31; sign/signifier, 31; in the *tonelle*, 19-20; trespassing of, 19, 51, 60

Braithwaite, E. K., 113

Broken phallus motif, 39, 63

Caribbean Contact, 71-72

Carnival, creation of, 28

Carter, Martin, 129

Ceremony of Souls, 13-14, 45; and the "dead" in society, 18-19; expressive of flux, 22. *See also* Tonelle

Characters, merging into one

About the Author

JOYCE JONAS is a Senior Lecturer in the Department of English at the University of Guyana. Her articles ''Anancy-strategies in *The Whole Armour*'' and ''Reflections on Reflections'' appeared in the journal *Kyk-over-al*, and ''Wilson Harris and the Concept of Threshold Art'' was published in the *Journal of West Indian Literature*.